CITIZENS LEGAL MANUAL

USING A LAWYER

. . . And What To Do If Things Go Wrong

HALT

Also by HALT:

Shopping for a Lawyer
Using a Law Library
Small Claims Court
Estate Planning
Probate
Real Estate
Divorce
Victims' Rights

Authors: Adrien Helm and Kay Ostberg
Editor: Richard Hébert
Special Research: Jeff Meyer, George Milko, Theresa Meehan
Graphics and Production: Bob Schmitt

*Our thanks to the following for their review, comments and advice in
the preparation of this manual:* Judith Doctor, Gerald Goldfarb,
Frank Jose, Leonard Kopelman, Theresa A. Meehan, David Ontell,
Caroline Stellman, Robert S. Tigner.

First Edition: October 1985
ISBN No. 0-910073-08-2

CONTENTS

INTRODUCTION

Using a Lawyer is a consumer guide for managing your business dealings with a lawyer. It provides practical advice about how to avoid problems with the lawyers you hire and how to fire or bring action against them if preventive steps fail.

HALT has published this manual to further its legal reform goals. Central to HALT's reform program is the belief that many legal problems can be solved by informed consumers *without* a lawyer. However, HALT also recognizes some form of professional help is necessary or desirable under some circumstances. In such cases, being informed will improve your chance of receiving good service and allow you to maintain full control of your legal affairs.

Lawyers sell legal services. As a customer, you choose the service you want to buy and come to an agreement on the terms of the purchase. You are the employer. It is your money, your property and your rights that are at stake. It is your responsibility to choose a lawyer carefully, to keep yourself informed about your case and to bring any problems to a lawyer's attention as soon as they arise. As with any purchase, you have the right to expect value for your dollar and to hold the seller to the terms of the purchase contract. This manual helps you do that.

It is organized chronologically. It begins with a discussion of alternative levels of client involvement, reviews advice on shopping for a lawyer and ends with strategies for redress if you have been a victim of attorney misconduct. The information ranges from the general, such as explaining the business nature of the relationship, to the detailed, such as suggesting how to maintain control over your records.

The final chapters explain what you can do if problems occur with your attorney. Suggestions for effective resolution short of formal grievance proceedings are discussed. If these fail, formal remedies are explored, including official grievance procedures, arbitrating fee disputes, client security trust funds and malpractice suits. Guidelines are given to help you understand each of these processes.

Appendix I suggests a model client-attorney contract; Appendix II shows the procedural stages of a typical civil suit, and Appendix III contains state-by-state information about grievance, arbitration and client security fund mechanisms.

A Word About Terms

This manual uses common, everyday language in the text. Where familiarity with a legal term can be helpful, the legal word or phrase is also included. The more acquainted you are with these few terms, the more confidently you will be able to negotiate the arrangements you want.

Appendix II includes a glossary of basic terms for procedures of a typical civil suit. Many of these terms do not appear in the text, but familiarity with them will help you understand your case proceedings.

How To Use This Manual

It's best if you read this manual through *before* hiring an attorney. It will give you a solid foundation upon which to build your client-attorney relationship.

If you already have a working relationship with a lawyer, the manual can still help you identify potential troublespots. As this manual explains, when trouble occurs, you should always act to modify the relationship. If nothing else, you can inform yourself about your legal concern, ask your lawyer or a second lawyer appropriate questions and become more actively involved in your case.

If you first pick up this manual *after* problems have developed with your lawyer, turn to the chapters that explain strategies for solving them. In those chapters, the manual discusses the most frequent types of client complaints, the pros and cons of firing an attorney and how to lodge a formal complaint against an attorney. They also tell you what to consider if you want to sue a lawyer for malpractice. In sum, the early chapters of the manual can be compared to preventive medicine, the latter to medical treatment or surgery.

Chapter 1:
CLIENT INVOLVEMENT

Clients who are fully informed are better equipped to make key decisions in their case, to avoid problems by spotting and solving them early on and to monitor their attorney's actions.

Consumers hire attorneys for two things: their expertise in legal procedures and their familiarity with *You ARE involved* the local courts and court personnel. You don't want your involvement to hinder your attorney from using the expertise you purchased, but you have no choice in the matter: you *are* involved. You are legally responsible for any actions your attorney takes in your name. The degree of active involvement you seek will affect the time and money you spend on a case and how well you are informed about actions taken.

As a client, you can be involved in your case at any of several different levels. You can handle your case on your own and use a lawyer only to review your paperwork, or you can use a lawyer in a more conventional way — hiring one to handle the entire case and give you progress reports. Between these two extremes are several other options as well. To determine which is most appropriate for you, you should educate yourself as much as you can about your case.

Learn about your kind of case Begin with a book that discusses your kind of legal problem. HALT and several other self-help publishers offer plain-language books on legal topics ranging from fighting traffic tickets to do-it-yourself divorces. Check with HALT and your local bookstores and public libraries for written resources prepared for nonlawyers. A law library can provide further education. HALT's **"Using a Law Library"** is a good step-by-step guide to legal research. You might also want to bring along a plain-language legal dictionary.

You should also be familiar with court procedures and the stages of a typical lawsuit. Appendix II guides you through these stages and defines the terms used at each step. Knowing these steps and the legal terms involved will make it easier for you to work with your lawyer. However, bear in mind that not every case involves all the stages of our model; don't feel something is wrong simply because some steps are omitted. In fact, most cases are settled out of court and never reach the trial stage.

You can also get information by talking to clerks at the courthouse or to staff of a government agency, legal aid office or a law school clinic. Not only are these people familiar with court procedures, they are used to dealing with nonlawyers, but don't be surprised if court clerks resist giving you information. Many of them are afraid of violating rules against nonlawyers giving legal advice. Also, other staff might be unwilling to talk with you because of heavy caseloads. Nevertheless, it is always worth a try.

Educating yourself about your case will help you answer four basic questions:

- How can using the legal system solve your problem?
- Do you want to handle the case on your own, using self-help materials?
- Do you want to use mediation or some other alternative to litigation to solve your problem?
- Do you want to hire an attorney?

Decide Your Lawyer's Role

If you do decide to hire an attorney, you can hire one as a *pro se* coach. You would be on record as representing yourself and would do the work on your case. The attorney would be paid an hourly fee to review your work or to coach you before a hearing or other court proceeding. If, for example, you own a small apartment building, you might know enough to take your own cases into court to enforce leases or collect bills, but want to hire an attorney to coach you on recent changes in the law or to review your court papers for accuracy.

Offer to do money-saving chores

If you decide to have an attorney do most of the work, you can still do work on the case that will save the lawyer's time and your money. You can volunteer to undertake tasks essential to your case that don't require a lawyer's specialized training. For example, you can run errands to get forms, search public records, research government regulations or compile data to support your case, data you are probably more familiar with than your attorney. These are only a few of the kinds of practical support you can give your lawyer. Propose money-saving alternatives to your lawyer whenever they occur to you, and ask the lawyer to suggest chores you can do to speed the case and lower your costs.

Legal problems aren't like broken pipes. You don't simply call a lawyer and say "fix it" unless you don't care how it is fixed or how much the repair costs. You hire an attorney because you want legal expertise, but you imperil your pocketbook and the outcome of your case if you adopt an attitude of "send me the bill." Whatever degree of involvement you decide on, it is essential to communicate to your attorney both your willingness and intention to be helpful and your ownership of the legal matter under consideration. If the relationship works right, you and your lawyer are partners working for a common goal — with you as the senior partner.

Chapter 2:

SHOPPING FOR A LAWYER

This chapter discusses the major techniques you can use in shopping for and choosing a lawyer. Careful shopping is important; it is your first and best opportunity to make sure you are hiring a lawyer in whom you have confidence and with whom you will be able to work. Comparative shopping for a lawyer helps you:

- Understand the range of services and prices available.
- Compare differing views on your legal problem.
- Select a lawyer who is likely to handle your case as you expect.

List Your Prospects

Your first step in hiring an attorney is to generate a list of prospects. Ask for recommendations from business acquaintances, relatives, friends, professionals such as clergy, counselors, social workers and physicians. The foundation of a good lawyer-client relationship is mutual respect, so you should solicit suggestions from people whose judgment you consider sound.

Ask for specific information

It is not enough to get an endorsement like "So-and-So is a fine lawyer." You need specific information about the kinds of problems the lawyer has handled and why the person is recommending this particular one. This will enable you to evaluate the recommendation in light of *your* problem and how *you* want to handle it.

You can also get names of attorneys from groups that provide legal services or work on issues related to your legal concern. These may be private organizations, government agencies, local bar associations, legal aid organizations or public interest groups. Such organizations often maintain lists of attorneys willing to accept referrals. Attorneys agree to be listed with them because of interest in a particular area of the law, because they are public-spirited, and because they want to generate business.

Get names from clinics, law schools

Law schools and private legal clinics are other sources of lawyer prospects. Many law schools operate legal clinics to give their students "real world" experience on legal cases under the supervision of attorneys. Most of these clinics serve clients with limited income and charge no fees. However, some law school clinics specialize by subject area and serve clients regardless of their income.

Private legal clinics are staffed by lawyers who handle large numbers of routine legal matters, such as will-drafting, lease-writing, uncontested divorces and bankruptcy. By accepting a large volume of repetitive business, these clinics are able to keep costs down and charge clients lower fees than most private law firms charge. Such clinics are listed in the Yellow Pages.

Check Yellow Pages, directories

The Yellow Pages and various directories that can be found in law libraries are also sources of lawyers' names. One directory, the *Martindale-Hubbell Law Dictionary*, is a well-known "Who's Who" of lawyers with brief biographical information provided by the lawyers themselves and a rating system. The ratings are of little practical help, however, because they are based on recommendations by fellow lawyers and not clients. *Martindale-Hubbell* does include specialty categories for attorneys, but be sure to read carefully the qualifications for declaring a specialty. Also, be careful to assess the information in any directory you look at by finding out first who put the information together and why.

Your search has just begun when you have compiled a list of names. You should use this list the way you would use a page of want ads for used cars. It is now time to contact the prospects you've identified and begin judging the quality of the services they offer for sale.

Initial Contact

Write down questions

Telephone each prospect. This initial contact will help you shorten your list. Prepare for the calls by writing down the questions you want to ask each lawyer. If you are well organized and know what you want to ask and how you want to ask it, you will save both yourself and the attorney time and demonstrate your intention and ability to remain in charge or your legal affairs in a businesslike, professional way.

Use the telephone call to:

1. Identify yourself and explain that you are hiring an attorney to help you with a case involving _____ .

2. Determine the cost, if any, for an initial consultation interview.

Ask questions that have simple answers

3. Ask any questions you think are important and which can be answered with yes or no or with other brief answers. For example, you can ask:

- Have you handled this kind of case before?
- Do you sign written fee agreements with clients?
- What are your usual rates for this type of case?
- Are your fees negotiable?
- How many years have you practiced?
- Can you refer me to clients for whom you've handled cases like mine?
- Do you usually represent any special interest groups, such as senior citizens?

4. Answer questions the attorney may have.

5. Ask about anticipated problems working on your case.

6. Schedule an in-person interview if the prospect still appears worth pursuing.

Be wary of lawyers who resist an interview

You can discover much from this sort of initial contact. If, for example, you are not allowed to talk with the lawyer who will be working on your case, this tells you something about how the office is run. The senior attorney may be the "salesperson" who is prepared for your questions. The junior attorney who will handle your case could be less experienced. If it is clear that the lawyer is unhappy that you want to conduct an interview before hiring, this could signal that this lawyer is not for you.

Don't feel bad if, after making several calls, you call back to cancel some appointments. Conducting more than three or four interviews will be time-consuming and probably unnecessary, so don't be shy about selecting only your "prime" candidates to interview.

The Interview

The interview is for finding out as much as you can about the lawyer. It is not the time to tell the attorney everything there is to know about your legal concern, but you do want to give enough information so the lawyer can accurately explain how it would be handled. You have three goals in this interview:

- To determine if the lawyer is experienced, able and willing to undertake your case.
- To understand what services will be performed for you and how much you will be charged for them.
- To learn whether you will be comfortable working with the lawyer.

10

Prepare for the interview by writing a brief summary of your case, including all relevant dates and all major facts. Your lawyer will need some of this information immediately and you will save time if it is prepared to present. Prepare a list of questions to ask the lawyers you interview. During the interview, make notes of the lawyer's answers so you can compare them when making your final choice.

Any questions you feel comfortable asking and which will elicit information pertinent to your goals will do, but don't wander too far afield from your primary objective — evaluating the lawyer's ability to handle your case. One further warning: don't be so pre-occupied with your "script" of questions that you forget to listen to the answers for both content and style.

It cannot be overemphasized that you are establishing a relationship which will work to the extent that you and the lawyer respect one another. Approach the interview seriously. Be businesslike, listen carefully and communicate accurately and with interest.

Chapters 3 and 4 of this manual cover employment and fee agreements. These are critical to discuss in your interview, because misunderstandings most often occur between lawyers and clients over expectations about service and fees that weren't clearly specified at the outset. The questions you ask in this area should give you a clear understanding of the lawyer's standard practice. Remember, at this point you have not decided to hire this lawyer.

Making a Decision

Immediately after each interview, review your notes to make sure they accurately reflect the exchange that occurred. Your notes will make it easier later on when it's time to make your choice.

When all interviews are completed, balance each lawyer's strengths and weaknesses, deciding which factors are most important to you and whether you have a clear choice.

For example, a lawyer newly admitted to the bar may be less expensive and quite capable of reviewing your simple will, but if you want help preparing a complex estate plan complete with several trusts, you probably want a seasoned tax and estate-planning specialist.

If you are suing a local lawyer, the most important factor may be to hire an out-of-town attorney, even though it means you will have to pay the lawyer's travel expenses.

If you are not satisfied, start over

If none of the lawyers you interview meets your needs, look for other prospects by drawing up a new list or going back to your old list and calling others to schedule interviews. Unless you are under extreme pressure to resolve your case quickly, it is far better to invest additional time at this stage than to try to undo a poor decision later.

Once you have made your choice, call the attorney and make an appointment to discuss employment and fee agreements, the subject of the next two chapters.

Chapter 3:

FEE ARRANGEMENTS

An employment agreement is a legally binding contract enforceable in court. It spells out the terms of your relationship with your lawyer and the fees you can be charged. The terms "agreement" and "contract" are used interchangeably in this manual, but if you don't have a *written* agreement, you will have no way to prove the terms of your agreement. It will be your word against that of your lawyer.

Before taking a case, many attorneys don't tell their clients how they calculate their fees. Others fail to document hours and expenses when they bill clients. Written fee agreements could prevent these problems, but such agreements are voluntary — and all too infrequent. It is up to you, the client, to make sure you have one with your lawyer, and that you *get it in writing*. The fact that fee disputes are the most common attorney-client problem should convince you of the benefits of written agreements. They can prevent misunderstandings, surprise expenses and overcharging.

An employment agreement should cover two things: fees and the terms of employment. This chapter discusses how fees are assessed, what services are covered and what is "extra." Chapter 4 covers the other terms of employment, including:

- *Retainers* — The amount you have to pay, how it will be used and whether it is refundable.

- *Expenses* — An estimate of the costs and how they are to be paid.

- *Billings* — How often itemized bills will be sent to you and when payments are due.

- *Timetable* — Estimates of the total time the

case will take and when each stage of work will be complete.

- *Conflict Resolution* — How disputes will be resolved, procedures for modifying the agreement and procedures to follow if you decide to terminate the lawyer-client relationship.

- *Responsibilities* — What the lawyer and you are each responsible for doing.

Insist on a written agreement

If the attorney you want to hire refuses to agree to a contract, it may be time to reconsider your choice of lawyers. It cannot be over-emphasized how important this agreement might be to you. In particular:

- It can prevent misunderstandings. ("I didn't know the expenses would be deducted *after* the attorney's third was taken out!")

- It can provide a measure of the attorney's conduct. ("I thought all attorneys billed at the end of the case, not every month!")

- It gives you written proof of your understanding.

- The attorney is aware that you will use the agreement to measure case progress and thus will be more likely to abide by the terms of the agreement.

The 'Reasonable' Fee

'Reasonable' can include a percentage fee

In the absence of a fee agreement to the contrary, the law allows an attorney to collect a "reasonable" fee. The definition of "reasonable fee" varies from state to state, but one of the factors often used to decide what is "reasonable" is the dollar value of the transaction involved. An attorney who has not signed a contract or who has included a vague "catch-all" clause in your contract can often claim a percentage of the settlement as a fee. Thus, the fee may not be based

14

only on the time spent or the difficulty of the work done.

Consider the divorce case of HALT member Sheila Cook. When she hired an attorney to help her work out her property settlement and other matters pertaining to her divorce, she did not have a fee agreement with her lawyer. She assumed the lawyer would be bound by a fair hourly fee. Imagine her surprise when she was billed $100,000 — the equivalent of $400 an hour, and her shock when a judge agreed that $75,000 of the charges was "reasonable" because of the amount of money involved in the property settlement. A written agreement could have prevented that.

Three Kinds of Fees

Few laws govern fees

It is important to understand the three main kinds of fees that lawyers charge and the incentives lawyers have for using each. Remember, it is up to you to negotiate the fee structure that suits you best. Few laws govern lawyers' fees. Those that do usually involve little more than setting a fee ceiling for certain types of cases. For example, a lawyer in New York can charge a maximum of 25 percent of the amount awarded in Social Security cases. In the absence of such laws, fee agreements are the consumer's only protection against excessive "reasonable" fees.

Hourly Fees

Lawyers bill for fractions of an hour

Hourly fees are based on the number of hours worked. If your lawyer charges $100 an hour, your fee will be $100 multiplied by the number of hours worked. Lawyers also bill for partial hours spent, usually by the quarter or tenth of an hour. For example, if your $100-an-hour lawyer charges in quarter hour increments, expect to be billed $25 for a five-minute telephone call.

Under an hourly-fee arrangement, the more hours worked, the bigger the bill. This rewards the lawyer who puts in more hours on your case, whether or not it needs that much time, and serves as an incentive to prolong cases rather than to bring them to a quick conclusion. This may not be in the client's best interest.

You can prevent "over-lawyering" by comparing your bills to the estimates you collected on the number of hours your case would take, including the estimate in your agreement. By checking your itemized bills, you can determine at each stage whether or not your lawyer is exceeding the hours expected. Whenever you suspect "over-lawyering," discuss it with your attorney.

If you agree to an hourly rate, you don't want to pay the attorney's hourly fee for typing done by a secretary, for a messenger delivering your documents across town, or for a law clerk looking up the laws involved in your case. Make sure that you know, and that your agreement specifies, the hourly rates you'll pay for support staff work.

Hourly rates are usually preferable to contingency fee arrangements (see below) because they are based on the time the attorney spends working on your case. However, you must watch for the attorney who is learning the law on your money and the one who sees your case as an opportunity to prolong a suit and bill you accordingly.

Flat Fees

Legal clinics and many lawyers now offer *flat fees* for routine legal matters, such as will preparation, incorporation of a business, lease preparation, some probate work, uncontested divorces and other uncomplicated matters. A flat fee means you will be charged a specified total for work on your case. For example, a lawyer might offer to prepare your will for $100, regardless how long it takes. Often, an agreement with a flat fee will require that the client also pay such "extras" as filing fees, photocopying and other out-of-pocket or unanticipated expenses.

16

Flat fees are charged when lawyers can accurately predict the average amount of time a case will take because the work usually can be completed by filling out standard forms or is almost identical to numerous other cases handled by the office. Recognize, however, that a flat fee reflects an hourly rate, so ask how much time the work will take, include this estimate in your agreement and choose an hourly figure if the math works in your favor. Usually, however, flat fees work out to be bargains because, when the work is repetitive and time-saving forms are used, the savings are passed on to the clients.

A *fixed maximum fee* is similar to the flat fee. Under this plan, you will be charged hourly; the total fee can be less but not greater than the fixed maximum. Any fixed maximum should be explained in your agreement.

Flat fees allow you to shop among lawyers if you have a routine matter. Ask the specifics about what the flat fee covers in each case to be sure the various attorneys are offering the same services for the quoted price. In other words, if one lawyer's flat fee includes typing and copying costs and another's identical fee does not, the first lawyer is more economical. If you agree to a flat fee, make sure your agreement specifies exactly what the fee covers and any costs that are not included.

Contingency Fees

Contingency fees are most common in personal injury or collection cases in which the client cannot afford to pay if the case is lost. If you win, your lawyer gets a percentage of the winnings; if you lose, the lawyer doesn't get paid. The theory behind contingency fees is simple: the attorney takes a risk of losing, the greater the risk, the bigger the percentage.

If you win, the attorney reaps a windfall on the theory that the attorney must also absorb a loss on the contingency fee cases that didn't succeed. However what usually happens is that lawyers get this windfall on most cases they handle because they rarely accept cases in which much, if any, risk is involved. Contingency fees are popular among lawyers in this country but are illegal in England, Canada, India and most of Europe.

Contingency fees illegal in many countries

The customary contingency fee is 33 percent of the settlement, although fees range from 25 to 50 percent. Some lawyers offer a sliding scale in which the percentage changes depending on the stage at which the case is settled. For example, the lawyer may collect 25 percent if you settle before trial, 30 percent if there is a trial and 40 percent if there is an appeal.

Although a sliding scale might seem attractive at first glance, be wary. If you agree to a sliding scale, your attorney may try to get you to accept settlement because going to trial involves more time and work, even though you would do better to continue pursuing the case. Also recognize that when you weigh a settlement offer, you will have to consider paying an additional 5 percent in attorney fees if you reject it and go to trial. So, if you accept a sliding scale geared to settlement, keep in mind that your interest and that of your attorney may not be the same as the case develops.

If a contingency fee arrangement is the only option available to you, follow these tips in negotiating your fee agreement with an attorney.

Tips for negotiating contingency fees

1. Find out how much the other person or the insurance company will offer you directly, without the help of an attorney.

2. Ask several lawyers to estimate your chances of success, how much you might be awarded and how many hours the case will take. Be suspicious of estimates that are far lower than others you've received. Ask the attorney if the fees are negotiable.

3. Using the estimates, calculate how much you can expect to receive after paying attorney fees and expenses. If it is about the same as was directly offered you, negotiate a settlement on your own.

4. If you decide to hire a lawyer, figure out the approximate hourly rate, based on your estimates. If it is substantially higher than the lawyer's regular hourly rate, bargain for one of these alternatives:

- A set hourly rate. This is particularly appropriate if you are sure of winning or you want the lawyer to serve as a consultant rather than handle the entire case.

- An hourly rate with an additional percentage amount if the lawyer wins substantially more than you were offered.

- A sliding scale based on the amount of the award. For example, 33 percent for the first $5,000, 25 percent for the next $5,000 and so on.

5. Ask that the percentage fee be calculated after expenses have been subtracted from the award. This can result in substantial savings. Consider the example in the accompanying box.

6. Set a limit on the amount of expenses you can be billed for. If more expense money is needed, make sure your agreement requires your lawyer to get your express approval.

CONTINGENCY FEE FIRST		EXPENSES FIRST	
Total Award	$90,000	Total Award	$90,000
Lawyer's Fee (1/3)	-$30,000	Less Expenses	-$12,000
Remainder	$60,000	Remainder	$78,000
Less Expenses	-$12,000	Lawyer's Fee (1/3)	-$26,000
NET TO YOU:	**$48,000**	**NET TO YOU:**	**$52,000**

Chapter 4

TERMS OF EMPLOYMENT

In addition to negotiating how your lawyer is going to calculate the fee, you must also negotiate the other terms of the client-lawyer relationship — whether you will have to pay a retainer; what expenses you will have to pay; when and how you will be billed; how much time the case will take and what reports of its progress will include so you can monitor developments; how conflicts between you and the lawyer will be resolved and, if they cannot be, how and under what circumstances you can fire your lawyer.

This chapter examines each of these employment contract provisions in turn and offers suggestions you may want to incorporate in your final agreement with your lawyer. In addition, Appendix I offers a model client-attorney contract you may want to use as a guide.

Retainers

The term "retainer" is often used imprecisely and can be a source of confusion. If you agree to any type of retainer, be careful that your agreement specifies what is meant.

Pure Retainers

These are fees paid to law firms to assure that a particular lawyer or firm will do all the client's work over a fixed period of time — typically a year. They are often used by businesses to secure the services of a particular lawyer or firm thought to be expert in a given field and to keep that lawyer or firm from representing competitors. Fees for work actually done are paid in addition to the retainer. The retainer generally is not refundable.

Case Retainers

These fees are paid to "retain" the services of an attorney at the beginning of a case. This is the kind of retainer most often paid by the typical legal consumer. It may represent all of the fee, none of the fee or a portion of it. It may be refunded or not, depending on your agreement.

Make clear what the retainer covers

For example, a lawyer may charge you a flat fee of $400 for an uncontested divorce and ask you to pay a retainer of one quarter — $100 — up front. This money may also be used to pay expenses associated with the case, such as filing fees. The important thing to make clear at the outset is whether the retainer is an advance on expenses, fees or both, and whether any unused part of it will be refunded.

General Representation Retainers

These retainers are used to cover a predictable level of legal work needed on a regular basis. They give businesses ready access to legal advice and routine services. The retainers are billed periodically and make the law firm readily available for work by telephone, review of documents or other volume work. Usually, such a retainer will *not* cover extraordinary legal projects like complex litigation and is not refundable.

Pre-Paid Legal Plans

'Pre-paids' work like retainers

Pre-paid plans often involve paying a set fee that is like a retainer. They resemble health maintenance organizations (HMO's) and, like those plans, cover certain kinds of work for a flat yearly rate. Common to both legal and medical service plans is the idea that a group of professionals agrees to serve a defined pool of consumers for a set annual fee. Pre-paid legal plans usually cover routine matters like wills, personal bankruptcy, employment concerns and tax preparation.

Expenses

In addition to fees, you will probably have to pay all the expenses or "costs" of your case. These can include court filing fees, fees for expert witnesses and money for transcripts, stenographers, copying, mailing, long distance telephone calls and transportation for out-of-town attorneys. If your case goes to trial, these expenses can be quite high.

'Advance against costs' covers expenses

You may be asked to pay an *Advance Against Costs* at the time you hire your attorney. Such advances are intended to cover expenses which arise in the course of the employment. As an advance, these fees should be refunded if not spent, but make sure that your agreement clearly specifies that they will be. Get a receipt so you will have a record of what has been advanced to compare against an itemized bill.

If you or your lawyer thinks the expenses in your case will be high, it is a good idea to set a limit on the amount of expenses you can be charged, based on your attorney's estimate. Then, if more needs to be set aside, your agreement can require your attorney to get your express approval.

Set a limit on expected expenses

Expert witnesses are particularly expensive but often necessary in complex lawsuits. Make sure you understand what you are paying for and why your attorney wants to hire the expert. Understand that the expert will cost you not only for the time spent testifying at trial, but for trial preparation, pre-trial questioning and travel. If you are told that the firm always uses a particular expert witness, ask about the firm's win-loss record using that expert's testimony and if there are less expensive alternatives.

Billing Arrangements

Billing arrangements should be spelled out in your agreement. Bills provide a history of your dealings with your lawyer and serve to spread payments out over a period of time. They also serve as a management tool for you because they remind the lawyer you expect periodic progress reports on your case and want to know all steps taken on your behalf.

Ask for monthly itemized bills

In most cases, you should ask for monthly itemized bills. If you anticipate long periods of inaction on your case, you can modify this requirement. You should ask that the itemization reflect the time spent on your case, what was done and all expenses to date. Remember, support staff hours should be listed separately from the attorney's hours. The more detailed your bill, the better you will understand what is happening on your case and how much money you are spending on it.

Most attorneys are willing to allow clients to pay in installments. If you think you will need to spread your payments out over a longer period than it is expected to take to resolve your legal problem, ask the attorney about this. Any arrangement you come to should be written into your agreement.

Timetable

Your agreement should estimate the total time the case will take and spell out the precise tasks the attorney will perform for you and how long they will take. The attorney may find the time difficult to predict, but even "ballpark" estimates will be extremely valuable to you.

Time estimates help judge progress

This timetable will allow you to judge the progress of your case. It should identify the logical stages of the case, likely to be the most convenient times for you to discuss with your lawyer such things as case progress and your degree of involvement in the process. If work is not proceeding on schedule, the timetable will reveal this and enable you to discuss it knowledgeably with the attorney to discover the reason and what, if anything, should be done about it.

Resolving Disputes

Agree how to resolve disputes

Remember the adage about "an ounce of prevention" when approaching the question of how you and your lawyer will resolve conflicts. It is important that you have discussed what mechanisms you will use if problems arise during the course of the attorney's employment. It is a difficult subject because it is much like writing a separation agreement on the eve of a wedding, but writing the terms of conflict resolution into your agreement can save you both time and money later on.

Specify no fee for time spent resolving conflicts

You can include a clause specifying that you and your attorney will agree to discuss openly all causes of dissatisfaction and seek reconciliation. You should specify that there will be no fee charged for time spent trying to resolve this dissatisfaction. You can specify that if this informal method of resolution fails, you will resolve the difficulty through more formal mechanisms, such as mediation or arbitration.

For example, you may be completely satisfied later with the quality of the work being done, but feel you are being unfairly billed. In such cases it would have been perfectly proper to have included in your agreement a clause specifying that any fee disputes would be settled by mediation or arbitration. You can also agree that other disputes will be settled through these mechanisms. The important thing to remember is that it is essential that the issue of conflicts be directly addressed by your agreement.

Attorney Withdrawal or Firing

Chapter 7 contains a full discussion of the pros and cons of firing your attorney and facts about attorney withdrawal. This chapter discusses terms concerning firing or withdrawal that you may want to include in your agreement with your lawyer.

Withdrawal can cause delay and expense

If your lawyer withdraws from your case before trial, it can cause you serious delay and cost considerable money to educate a new lawyer about your case, so include in your agreement a provision that your lawyer cannot withdraw without 14 days notice or within 30 days of trial, except for extreme reasons such as illness or death. Include a provision that the attorney cannot withdraw if the withdrawal will significantly affect the outcome of imminent proceedings or if a competent lawyer cannot be found as a replacement. Require that if the attorney wants to withdraw, the withdrawal must be in writing and include the reasons for the withdrawal. This can be important if you decide to file a grievance or pursue a malpractice action later on.

You may have to pay for work done

Recognize also that, unless you provide otherwise in the agreement, when your lawyer withdraws or is fired, you will have to pay for the work done. The only exception to this rule is if you can prove you fired your attorney for "good cause." (See Chapter 7 for a list of "good cause" reasons.) In negotiating the terms of employment with your attorney, try to agree on payments in the event the attorney is fired. Write these terms into your agreement.

In some states, your attorney can keep some of your case documents (place a "lien" on them) if the attorney believes you owe money. This is likely to create problems if you choose to pursue your case, so make sure your agreement specifies that *all* documents pertinent to your case will be turned over to you immediately if your attorney is no longer handling the case.

Rights and Responsibilities

*include specifics
in your
involvement*

The way you've selected your attorney and prepared an agreement has demonstrated to that attorney how involved you want to be in the progess of your case. If you plan on working with the attorney throughout the case, it should be no surprise that you also want to include in the agreement specifics about your involvement.

Your agreement should specify your lawyer's rights and responsibilities as well as yours: who is to do what and when. The agreement should spell out how you expect to participate in the case and what you expect of your attorney. For example, this section of your agreement might specify that you expect regular updates on your case, or that you will file all documents with the courts and take care of locating witnesses.

Conclusion

*insist on plain
language*

Written agreements benefit both you and the attorney by providing a concrete understanding of the terms of your relationship and the expectations on both sides. Make sure you understand this agreement before signing it. Insist on language you understand. Make it clear that you take the terms seriously because you are entrusting the attorney with concerns and interests which *belong to you*.

Chapter 5:

WORKING WITH A LAWYER

As stated earlier, you can't simply hand your problem over to a lawyer and sit back waiting for results unless you don't care about those results or the cost. Regardless of the degree of involvement you choose, you have certain responsibilities. Certain decisions can be made by no one but you. In addition to these minimal responsibilities, you can use basic strategies to avoid misunderstandings, create a reliable record of your relationship and spot problems early. Throughout this chapter, two pieces of advice are repeated often:

- Use your attorney's time efficiently.
- Get it in writing.

Your Responsibilities

You are in a position to require that your attorney behave responsibly toward you if you fulfill these basic client responsibilities.

Do What You Promise. If you have committed yourself to do certain tasks, perform them completely and promptly. Review and pay bills when they are due.

Tell your lawyer all the facts

Be Candid. Your lawyer can't operate effectively with half the facts. Anything important to your case will most likely come out in the end. Your lawyer is better off knowing what to expect and not being "blind-sided." Also, your candor and cooperation can breed candor and cooperation on the part of the lawyer.

Keep Your Lawyer Informed. This means updating the lawyer on events that affect your case. It also means letting your lawyer know if you omitted any important information in prior consultations.

Management Strategies

You can use any of the strategies discussed below to keep up-to-date on developments and your lawyer's actions. These strategies can save you time and money as well as provide early warning of problems.

Preparation

Organize facts, documents, questions for meetings

Collect all relevant documents and organize a short written summary of facts or questions before you meet with your attorney. This can save time for both of you. It also helps you make sure your questions get answered and that the discussion is focused.

Keep Notes

Date your notes

Make notes about what you want to discuss. This gives you a convenient way of keeping track of your talks with your attorney. Jot down the lawyer's answers on the same paper and date your notes. This creates a record to refresh your memory or to use if problems develop.

Keep Files

As soon as you have hired your attorney, set up a file for case documents. Keep a copy of your *signed* agreement, bills, a record of payments with the check or money order numbers noted, copies of all court papers or reports relevant to your case and your notes or letters about discussions with your attorney.

Keep originals of case documents

In a second file, keep your original case documents. The only times your lawyer is likely to need

28

originals is to use them as evidence in a trial or to transfer property ownership. Except at these times, you should keep all originals and give copies to your lawyer. This file will prove useful to both you and the lawyer for ready reference and, if problems arise with your attorney, you will not find yourself trying to hire another attorney at the last minute without the documents from your case file (see Chapter 7).

Write Letters of Understanding

Clients often complain about the length of time it takes to settle their case. Sometimes delay is the result of the court system, but at other times the delay is caused by the lawyer. One way to keep your lawyer's "feet to the fire" is to send letters of understanding. These restate the major points of your latest meeting or telephone conversation.

Be brief, restate decisions on tasks

Keep the letter brief and outline the basic decisions, how tasks are divided and the timetable agreed upon. Make the letters sound as though you are confirming your understanding of the arrangements, not as though you distrust the lawyer. Be sure to keep a copy of these letters and your lawyer's answers, if any, as they provide you with a written record of your case history.

For example, if during your office visit your lawyer tells you of plans to search for an important expert witness and that you should collect certain documents and meet in a week to prepare questions for the witness, you might follow up such a meeting with a letter like this:

August 30, 1985

Dear Lawyer McDougall:
I want to make sure I understood our conversation of March 29, 1985, so I'm putting it in writing. Please have your secretary

call me if there is any misunderstanding on my part.

You advised me that an orthopedic surgeon's testimony is more likely to produce a settlement than would the testimony of a chiropractor, although it will be three times as expensive. I am to collect all my doctor and therapy bills and be in your office next Wednesday at 1:00 p.m. You will collect the names and fee estimates of expert witnesses by then and we will draft our questions at that time.

Sincerely,

Samantha Client

Use the Telephone

Telephone consultations can be more economical than personal visits because you are more likely to get right to the point if you call. Also, you will not have to spend work time getting to your lawyer's office.

Keep in mind that your lawyer is probably billing you for telephone time and that a five-minute call may translate into a quarter of an hour of billed time. Also, your lawyer may not answer interruptive, unscheduled phone calls, particularly if the lawyer is in the middle of another client's consultation or trial. To use your time best and your lawyer's time most efficiently, follow these rules:

Phone rules for best results

- Call only when you have specific business.

- Ask if it is a convenient time to talk. If not, discuss how long your conversation will take and make an appointment. Ask the attorney to call you at the scheduled time.

- Keep your line clear. Be as punctual about this appointment as you would be if you were meeting in person.

- Keep a log noting when you talked and for how long. This can be compared with your itemized bill or serve as evidence should a grievance or fee dispute arise later.

- Follow-up your conversation with a letter of understanding.

Ask Questions

Answers lead to informed decisions

Don't nag, but don't be afraid to ask questions, either. It's the only way to get answers and be sure you understand exactly what is happening on your case. This is critical if you are to make key decisions and to understand your lawyer's reasoning. You may find that your lawyer's answers to your questions lead you to provide information you had not thought important earlier. Questions are critical, but they should be used not as weapons but as tools for informing both of you about the problem you are working together to solve.

Get Second Opinions

When you face an important decision in your case and are unsure why your attorney is recommending one course of action, such as accepting a settlement offer, think about getting a second opinion. You won't want to ask for second opinions over every decision in your case because they can be expensive, but you should be aware that they can be used effectively at almost any point in a case.

Look for the right lawyer. It won't do you any good to find someone who is unwilling to examine a fellow-lawyer's advice or who is looking to take over the case. You should explain the decision or action you want advice about and be clear that you are not trying to second-guess your attorney. You want only to inform yourself about other opinions and options.

Second opinions can be valuable but should only be sought and used when you have serious questions about what your lawyer is encouraging you to do. If you find yourself thinking about getting them more than once or twice, it may be time to consider hiring a new lawyer instead.

Consider Settling Early

If your lawyer's conduct is beginning to worry you, it may be time to consider settling your case. You need to balance the possible expenses and fees of going forward against the latest settlement offer made by the other side. If you have lost confidence in your attorney, it may be less costly for you to cut your losses.

Fighting AND switching can be expensive

Settling before you get what you wanted may seem like a bitter pill to swallow but, if your problems with your attorney worsen, the cost of switching lawyers or continued quarreling with the one you have may outweigh the amount you can get by pursuing your suit.

Of course, there are steps you can take *before* problems become so serious you have to consider settling early and dropping your case. The next chapter discusses these strategies.

Chapter 6:

IF PROBLEMS DEVELOP

An early talk can solve problems

If problems develop between you and your lawyer, respond to them *as soon as you become aware of them*. Don't ignore them and hope they will go away. If you do, they're more likely to get worse. An early talk with your lawyer can often solve everything and save you increased worry and frustration. Remember, communicate your concerns. Neither you nor your lawyer is a mind reader.

The most common complaint clients have about their lawyers is overcharging, followed by neglect of the client or case. Because of the frequency of complaints in these two areas, they are discussed at length in this chapter, but remember, the techniques you use to solve these problems can be used to solve others as well.

Fees and neglect are common problems

Examples of other problems you can run into include the lawyer's failure to contact your witnesses, failure to show up for a hearing or trial, failure to prepare you for a hearing, suggesting that you perjure yourself, agreeing to a settlement without your permission, pressuring you to make a decision, stealing your money and "blackmailing" you to pay additional fees immediately before trial. All such complaints, and others, often can be successfully dealt with using the strategies discussed in this chapter.

Excessive Fees

Use written agreement to resolve disputes

A written agreement that is clear about your lawyer's fees can prevent fee disputes from escalating. You can use the terms of your agreement as a tool to resolve difficulties. For example, if you agreed on a monthly itemized billing and no bill arrives, you can

33

call and ask about the expected bill. This way you are both seeking to solve the problem and telegraphing your seriousness about the agreement.

Overcharging

Itemized bills can reveal overcharging

If you did take the precaution of negotiating an agreement, your first bill should not be a surprise to you. If it seems significantly higher than what you expected, you may have been charged too much for the work done. Your key to understanding whether a fee is excessive is an itemized list of what has been done, the time it took and who performed the work — a paralegal, a clerk, a secretary or your laywer. All charges for expenses should also be itemized. If you don't have an itemized bill, write or call the lawyer and ask for one. Mention, too, that all future bills should be itemized.

Overlawyering

If you are surprised by an itemized bill because of the number of hours billed, the number of procedures required, the number of phone calls made by support staff or the amount of research time spent on your case, you may be a victim of "overlawyering." Such surprises may or may not have been your lawyer's fault, but your lawyer should have at least discussed with you in advance any developments that were likely to increase the cost of your case.

Overlawyering most commonly occurs in hourly-fee cases handled by large firms in which a senior lawyer serves as a business manager at the top of a pyramid of associate attorneys, paralegals, clerks, librarians, secretaries and other staff. These senior partners draw business to the firms and supervise the work of others. Such a system has built-in incentives for generating income through unnecessary work. Be mindful, however, that there is no guarantee small firms or solo practitioners will not overcharge or "overlawyer" as well.

Write a Letter

If, after careful review of your bill, you conclude that you have been overcharged, write a letter to your attorney challenging specific items that seem unnecessary. You should be firm but indicate a willingness to compromise. Suggest a specific dollar amount you consider fair. It is to your advantage to be reasonable and willing to negotiate.

Be brief, objective and focused

In your letter, remind the lawyer about estimates, what was said about fees earlier, or what seems fair to pay for your kind of case. Be businesslike. The best business letters recognize the value of the reader's time. They are to the point, logical, brief and objective. Stay focused on the central issues. You want your letter to be thoughtful and concise, not confrontational or disjointed. Keep a copy of the letter in your files.

Ask for a written response

If you write a letter, ask for a written response by a certain date. Two weeks is usually reasonable. Lawyers take the written word seriously. They appreciate the value of a written record and its weight in any legal arena. By using it, you are meeting them on their own ground, communicating the business attitude you bring to the relationship and creating a record, or "paper trail," should you need to take the case to fee arbitration or court later on. Your lawyer will be impressed.

Two Who 'Won'

When one HALT member took issue with the number of hours she was billed for her case, she wrote the law firm a letter outlining her understanding of the quantity, quality and nature of the legal services she had received. She explained what she believed to be the fair value of the services, based on the firm's hourly rate of $120, then added an extra percentage to show her "good faith." She suggested cutting the original bill by 25 percent. The firm accepted her offer.

In another case, a HALT member was charged $34,000 for legal services on a property sale. After receiving the bill, he asked for an accounting of the hours spent on the case. It turned out the firm had spent 112 hours on his case and charged $14,000 for this time at the firm's normal rate of $125 an hour. The additional $20,000 charge had been based entirely on the value of the property sold in the transaction.

Because there was no initial agreement on fees, the law allowed the firm to collect what was "reasonable." If the man took his dispute to court, he was likely to lose. The judge probably would rule that a "reasonable" fee included consideration for the value of the property sold (see Chapter 3). Nevertheless, the man wrote to the lawyer pointing out that:

- He had never agreed to pay a "reasonable fee" based on the legal definition of "reasonable."

- He had never agreed to pay an amount based on the value of the transaction.

- Much of the "value" the firm claimed to have delivered was part of the original, agreed-upon work and not an unexpected "windfall" or "bonus."

- He would accept the firm's statement of hours without question.

- He would allow the firm the highest rate that had been mentioned in their discussions — $125 an hour.

He proposed a compromise of $14,000. His lawyer wrote back:

As I have indicated earlier, I feel that our bill was quite reasonable at $34,000. However, it is clear that there was misunderstanding with regard to the basis of our fee. It is my view that in such a situation, the blame must rest with the lawyer. Therefore, I feel that I must agree with your offer of $14,000.

*Get a new
written bill*

If you and your lawyer do agree to a compromise, make sure a new bill is issued to reflect your agreement. Also, use this opportunity to discuss what you should do if other problems occur between you. This will show your commitment to an ongoing working relationship.

If you still cannot come to an agreement after sending letters and telephoning, you may want to take your disagreement to formal fee arbitration, or even consider firing your attorney. If so, see Chapter 7 on firing and Chapter 8 on fee arbitration.

If Your Lawyer Neglects You

The second most common complaint against attorneys is neglect. Either the lawyer fails to return telephone calls, fails to meet deadlines, ignores your letters, repeatedly forgets critical facts of the case or passes you on to a clerk or paralegal each time you call or visit the office.

*Reasons for
delays should
be explained
in advance*

As stated earlier, some delays are beyond the control of attorneys. They are built into the court system in the interest of being fair to all sides. Nevertheless, as with unexpected fees, the reason for an unexpected delay should at least be made clear to you as soon as it is foreseen.

However, if your case is delayed because your lawyer simply hasn't gotten around to it, you are justified in being upset. If you've been told that certain things will be done in two weeks and they are not done in three, your lawyer owes you an explanation. If a filing date is approaching and you've heard nothing from your lawyer, you have grounds to worry.

*First complaint:
use the phone*

The first time such a situation occurs, telephone and tell your lawyer about your concerns. Mention the timetable in your employment agreement, if you have one. Be organized and brief. Explain that you wish to discuss only your concern about the neglect, not the case itself, and that you do not expect to be billed for the time involved. Note the call in your log. Make the contact friendly and relaxed, but be firm about your concern and its seriousness.

Second complaint: write a letter

If the problem occurs a second time, put your complaint in writing and mention your previous phone call. Keep a copy. The letter will be useful if problems persist and you want to file a grievance or malpractice case against the lawyer. Remember to ask for an answer by a specific date.

Don't accuse the lawyer in your letter, but be straightforward. Saying "I expected a bill which itemized all the charges," or asking "Is there a reason why such and such has not yet been completed?" are far less combative and far more likely to get results than more confrontational statements, such as "You were supposed to send me an itemized bill" or "You are late in completing. . ." Be cooperative but firm, until you decide your only recourse is to fire the attorney.

Multiple Problems

Talk problems over on neutral ground

If several serious problems have developed over time, schedule an appointment. Tell the lawyer in advance that you want to discuss how the relationship is working, that you don't want to be charged for the time, and that you want to meet on neutral ground.

In this meeting, encourage a candid exchange about your expectations that are not being met. You may both feel comfortable with modifying your agreement, writing one if you hadn't already done so or ending the employment. However, be careful about letting the lawyer go if doing so will jeopardize your case or leave you facing a long delay.

The Expectations Game

When judging your lawyer's work against your expectations, make sure you aren't falling prey to the following common misperceptions:

Your lawyer should be your friend. Clients often have to reveal intimate facts, feelings or thoughts to their lawyers, information normally revealed only to close relations and friends. However, don't make the mistake of thinking such confidences turn your lawyer into your best friend. Remember, this is a business relationship. If your lawyer becomes your friend outside your employment relationship, fine. But don't expect or rely on this "friendship" in dealing with your legal concern. You're paying your lawyer for legal expertise, not sympathy.

You're being "sold out." Some clients believe that because their lawyer is urging them to settle out of court, the lawyer has been bought by "the enemy." Settlement does not mean you've "lost." Remember, most cases are settled before trial. You hired your lawyer to assess the strengths and weaknesses of your case and give advice about alternatives. If your lawyer urges you to settle, it may be because the lawyer knows that the cost of pursuing the case outweighs the probable benefits.

If your attorney recommends settlement, ask for a comparison of the costs and likely benefits of pursuing the case further. It's best to get this in writing, too. *Don't ever accept a settlement offer unless you understand it fully and have read the settlement agreement carefully.* If you have doubts, don't sign until they are cleared up.

If you lose, it's your lawyer's fault. This may be the case, but don't assume it is. Paying for legal representation doesn't guarantee you will "win." Sometimes a case is weak and the odds are against your "winning." If so, mediation may get you a better settlement than a lawsuit. Sometimes the law or its interpretation changes, and what your lawyer believed was a strong case is abruptly weakened by court action a few days before your trial. Sometimes judges make mistakes or misapply the law despite a lawyer's best efforts.

In fact, the system of courtroom litigation almost guarantees the opposite of victory: that someone will "lose." All clients think their case is water-tight, that they are in the right and deserve to win. They believe the courts exist to give them all they are due. The difficulty is that this is true on both sides of every argument, and it is impossible for both sides to get everything they want. As a result, taking a case into court involves risk: in effect, you are asking someone else to decide what is right for you, instead of forging a solution yourself through compromise or negotiation.

It'll be over in a month. Lawyers aren't magicians. They are caught in the same crowded court backlogs and built-in procedural delays as you are. Hiring a lawyer in most cases won't speed up the process. In some situations, such as writing a will, drafting a lease or settling a real estate sale, a month may be reasonable but few other legal matters allow for such speedy resolution, whether you hire a lawyer or not. Your case will *never* be over in a month if it involves litigation or a hearing, and some civil cases do not reach trial until five years after the complaint was filed.

Negotiate Your Differences

If strategies for managing your attorney-client relationship fail and you are still faced with problems, try resolving them through negotiation. The most successful negotiators are organized, present themselves convincingly and have prepared a compromise position. Unless you are ready to fire your attorney, appear cooperative. After all, you are still hoping the lawyer will continue to work on your case and produce the results you want.

Don't Threaten To Sue

You may decide you want to sue your lawyer for malpractice or file a grievance (see Chapters 8 and 9).

Regardless of this decision, threatening such actions is not an effective way of getting a lawyer to "shape up." Instead, threats are likely to cause an irreparable rift. Besides, it can take three years or more for the suit or grievance complaint to be settled, and your lawyer knows it. Time will be on the lawyer's side, not yours.

If you have reached such an impasse, it is time to consider firing your lawyer or dropping your case. Instead of threatening to sue, put your reasons for preparing to fire your lawyer in writing and state that you will fire the lawyer unless the problem is solved. Specify the actions you want your attorney to take in order not to be fired. But remember, only when your efforts at negotiating have failed is it time to consider the more drastic step of firing your lawyer.

Chapter 7:

PARTING WITH A LAWYER

A client can fire an attorney, but an attorney can't "fire" a client. That is how it is supposed to work. The lawyer can, however, withdraw under certain conditions. Indeed, lawyers are *required* to withdraw from a case if they find they cannot represent their client competently.

Each state has different laws about this, but common reasons for requiring lawyers to withdraw include poor health, prior commitments to other cases that interfere with their ability to give attention to yours, conflict of interest and personal problems, such as alcoholism or marital stress. Attorneys can also withdraw from your case if you don't pay your bill or if you refuse to "cooperate," for example by not showing up for a meeting or by concealing facts essential to the case.

Practically, lawyers can withdraw anytime

Despite the consumer protection implied in these laws, their practical effect is that lawyers can withdraw almost anytime they choose. If no lawsuit has been filed, your lawyer can withdraw simply by telling you so. After a lawsuit has been filed, the lawyer must ask the court's permission before withdrawing, but such motions to withdraw are almost always approved by the court. They are denied only in extreme circumstances, such as when trial is scheduled the next day and your lawyer has already been granted several postponements.

If your lawyer asks you to agree to a withdrawal, weigh whether you want to file a lawsuit or formal complaint against the lawyer. If you do, you are better off not consenting to the withdrawal, even though chances are the court will allow the lawyer to drop your case anyway.

Whether or not you agree, ask the lawyer to send you a written notice of intent to withdraw and to state the reasons. (It's best if you included a requirement for this in your original employment agreement.) If your lawyer refuses to give you written notice, make a note of the time and date of the oral notice and include notes on the reasons given. This way you will have a record should you decide later to file a grievance with the bar or to sue your lawyer, discussed in Chapters 8 and 9.

When lawyers are allowed to withdraw, most states require them to help you find a new lawyer, to cooperate with your new attorney, to refund costs or fees which have not been earned and to return your case file. Despite these requirements, however, lawyers rarely volunteer to do any of these things. If you want them done, you'll probably have to assert your rights.

Firing Your Lawyer

Your freedom to fire your lawyer is almost absolute. You are not required to have a good reason. The only time you are not allowed to fire your lawyer is when you attempt to use the firing to delay a court proceeding or otherwise to manipulate a delay for your benefit.

The fact you are free to fire your lawyer doesn't mean you should use that freedom at the first sign of minor disagreement. You should carefully consider what firing your lawyer can cost you. The further along your case is, the more serious a step firing becomes. It will cost time and money and can seriously jeopardize your case. It should be considered only after you've tried to remedy your problems with the lawyer and in cases of serious misconduct. There are three major reasons *not* to fire a lawyer:

- Hiring and educating a new lawyer about your case is usually time-consuming and expensive.

- You may not find another lawyer willing to take the case.
- Delay may irreparably damage your case, for example by forcing you to miss critical deadlines.

Find a new lawyer BEFORE firing

It's a good idea to shop for a new lawyer *before* firing your old one. This way you'll know you won't have to drop the case or represent yourself. Any lawyer you interview will ask if you already have representation. Tell the truth: that you are dissatisfied with your present attorney and why. This may make some attorneys wary of taking your case, but your honesty can prevent the same kind of problems arising with your next attorney.

Consider getting a second opinion

Before firing your lawyer, talk over your concerns to make sure you understand the lawyer's side. If you are not sure whether you should fire the lawyer, consider getting a second opinion. Ask a staff person at the local bar grievance committee (see Appendix III). You may even want to ask another lawyer. It costs money to hire another lawyer to review your original lawyer's conduct, but you do need to make an informed decision.

Firing for 'Good Cause'

You may not owe fees

Although you can fire your lawyer for almost any reason, state laws also set out "good cause" reasons for firing. If you have such reasons, you may not have to pay fees. Most "good cause" reasons are also grounds for discipline or a malpractice suit against your lawyer. The laws differ from state to state, but most of them include the following "good cause" reasons:

Neglect. For example, your lawyer repeatedly misses deadlines and hearing dates and refuses to answer letters or return telephone calls.

Breach of Confidentiality. For example, after you have discussed with your lawyer your suspicions about your spouse's infidelity, you discover the lawyer has talked about those suspicions with fellow country club members.

Illegal Action. For example, your lawyer tells you to lie about your case under oath, or suggests that you bribe a witness.

Failure To Supervise Staff. For example, a casual acquaintance of yours is told about your divorce by your lawyer's secretary.

Incompetence. Your lawyer's actions reveal a pattern of repeated errors, such as failure to file court papers on time, having to refile papers that were incorrectly completed or filed, failure to learn current law related to your case, repeatedly trying to use inadmissable evidence, failure to call witnesses, being unprepared at hearings or settlement conferences, or missing the deadline for filing suit.

Morally Offensive Behavior. Some examples: your lawyer sexually harasses you; swears at you, the judge, your opponent or the other lawyer; or arrives drunk at hearings, settlement conferences or appointments. Simple rudeness is not considered "good cause" for firing a lawyer, however.

Conflicts of Interest. For example, your lawyer agrees to a settlement you did not approve, or has a personal financial interest that conflicts with your case. However, having lunch with your opponent's attorney does not constitute a conflict of interest.

Breach of Fiduciary Duty. When you entrust money or property, including your legal rights, to your lawyer, the lawyer is said to have a "fiduciary" duty to you. That duty is breached if, for example, your lawyer invests your daughter's trust fund in an extremely risky venture or fails to remind you to rewrite your will after major changes in your state's inheritance tax laws. Given the trust you have placed in your attorney, any significant failure to exercise good judgment qualifies as a breach of fiduciary duty.

Code of Ethics Violations. Each state bar has what is called a "Code of Professional Responsibility" or "Model Rules of Professional Conduct" that governs lawyers' behavior. Examples of typical violations: your lawyer puts your trust funds in a private bank account, is convicted of a felony, lies on a license application, or uses knowledge about your case to represent your opponent later on.

Don't pay disputed fees

If you have considered the pros and cons and have decided to discharge your lawyer, write a letter stating your reasons and schedule a meeting to discuss them. Make arrangements for paying the final bill if you agree that you owe the lawyer money. If you disagree with the lawyer over how much you owe and the lawyer threatens to keep your file if you don't pay, remember that paying now may get your files back but it will probably make it more difficult to negotiate a fee reduction or to get the lawyer to agree to fee arbitration later on. The best thing is to have preserved all your options in fee disputes by keeping your own file of all original documents from the beginning.

Chapter 8:

REDRESSING GRIEVANCES

People who have been the victims of attorney misconduct frequently ask HALT what they can do about it. All too often, the answer is, not much. Such people have four recourses:

- If the lawyer stole the client's money, the client can seek reimbursement from the state's Client Security Fund.
- If the client wants the lawyer disciplined for misconduct, a grievance complaint can be filed with the state or local bar.
- If the lawyer's fee is disputed, the client can ask for fee arbitration.
- Finally, the client can sue the lawyer for malpractice.

Firing your lawyer isn't required

You do not have to fire your attorney in order to have access to any of these recourses. You may use them even after the lawyer has successfully provided the services you bought. Your degree of satisfaction with the outcome may influence whether or not you seek formal remedies for complaints you have about your attorney, but you should never let that final outcome be the only determining factor. While the four options may seem, at first glance, to provide considerable remedies, several factors keep them from being of major benefit to most consumers.

Redress systems are run by lawyers

First, lawyers are self-regulating. State and local bar associations run the attorney grievance committees, client security funds and fee arbitration panels. Thus, each option for consumer redress involves submitting your complaint primarily to other attorneys. In most cases, the bar operates in secrecy and your right to appeal is limited. Of late, these and other bar programs to protect consumers have come under increasing public scrutiny and pressure for reform.

Assess all options

This is not to say that the procedures already in place aren't worth pursuing. If you believe you have been the victim of attorney misconduct, you should fully explore all your options. Remember, using one recourse doesn't prevent you from using one or more of the others. In fact, in some instances you may want to arbitrate a lower fee, seek reimbursement of stolen money from the client security fund, file a grievance complaint with the bar *and* file a malpractice suit. This chapter explains the pros and cons of pursuing the first three options — those administered by the state bars themselves. The next chapter discusses malpractice lawsuits.

Client Security Trust Funds

Bars reimburse money stolen from clients

One of the clearest cases of attorney misconduct is stealing a client's money. Because such theft is obviously flagrant misconduct and erodes public confidence in attorneys, state bar associations have established Client Security Funds. Money for these funds is collected from attorneys in the state, typically as part of their bar dues, and used to reimburse clients.

Lawyers can steal from clients in a number of ways. Most often, an attorney responsible for the money in a trust fund or an estate keeps it — or "comingles" it — with personal money. In one dramatic case, a New York attorney stole more than $1.5 million in this way from more than 100 clients before being discovered.

In other thefts, an attorney may accept a retainer fee but never do any work on a case and refuse to refund the money. Or an attorney may simply pocket the money won in a lawsuit. This is easily done, because attorneys generally have settlement checks made payable to them so they can deduct their fees before forwarding the remainder to you.

To be reimbursed for money stolen or misappropriated by your lawyer, simply apply to your state bar's Client Security Fund (see below). However, recognize that there is a limit on the amount refundable. The maximum that will be refunded on a single case varies from state to state. It can be as low as $5,000 or as high as $25,000. If your loss exceeds the limit, your only recourse to get the rest back is to sue the lawyer. This may be impossible or pointless, however, because by the time you become aware of the theft, your lawyer is likely to have fled the state or gone bankrupt.

Filing a Trust Claim

To file a claim, contact your state's fund committee (see Appendix III) and ask for the rules for filing. Usually, you cannot hire a lawyer to help you file your claim because lawyers are not allowed to accept payment for helping present a claim. You will be asked to fill out a form. You should attach copies of any letters, bills, or receipts and a brief summary of the complaint. Keep a copy of your form and the originals of any attachments you submit.

The fund committee is composed only of lawyers. They review your claim and contact the lawyer in question. They may also ask you to supply further information. No hearing is held, and the claim and evidence are not made public. If your claim is found to have merit, the committee orders reimbursement, but it reserves the right to reimburse only part of the money stolen. In most states, you can't appeal the committee's decision. If the committee turns you down or only partially reimburses you, your only recourse is to file a lawsuit against your lawyer.

If your claim is rejected, you will receive a letter advising you of the rejection, but depending on your state's rules, you may not have the right to have the reasons for the committee's decision stated in writing. In some states, if you have also filed a disciplinary complaint against your lawyer, the claim to the security fund will be delayed until the disciplinary complaint is settled. Also, information from the disciplinary committee can affect the outcome of your fund claim.

During its first 10 years, California's fund paid out up to 67 percent of claims each year, and typical claims ranged between $2,500 and $5,000. The state bar associations' unreviewable authority to administer these funds is coming under increasing challenge, but until payments from the fund are viewed as a right and not distributed by the "grace" of the bar, to quote the California rules, these challenges are unlikely to succeed. You have nothing to lose by seeking compensation from the fund, but be aware of the limitations.

Fee Arbitration

Most state and many local bar associations have established fee arbitration programs in response to the large number of fee complaints they receive (see Appendix III), but to date, the American Bar Association has not formally studied the issue or prepared model recommendations to the state and local bars.

The advantages of taking a disputed fee to arbitration is that it is quick, it is considerably less expensive than taking the dispute to court, and almost half the states with fee arbitration programs require that at least some nonlawyers serve on hearing panels. Of equal importance, if your lawyer takes you to court to collect a fee and wins, you could end up paying the costs, including your lawyer's own attorney fees.

Before your case is accepted for fee arbitration, the bar will want both you and your lawyer to agree to it. Your lawyer is more likely to agree to arbitration if you owe money than if you contend you have overpaid and want your money refunded. Thus, if you disagree with your lawyer's bill, think twice before paying it. Be sure you're right and can prove it, however, because if your lawyer refuses to submit to arbitration and instead sues you for payment, you could end up paying more than just the disputed fee.

If you have a dispute over your lawyer's bill and want to try arbitration, call your area bar office to learn:

- Are arbitration hearings formal? If the procedure is too formal, you may not want to handle it on your own. On the other hand, formality can mean the panel is serious about its operation and that cronyism is kept to a minimum.

- Is there a formal administrative structure and someone in charge of the operation? Make sure that what goes under the banner of "arbitration" is not simply "mediation" in another lawyer's office — a signal that cronyism may be at play.

- Are there incentives to encourage lawyers to agree to arbitrate? For example, the Fee Arbitration Board in Washington, D.C., provides an attorney to represent you in court if your attorney refuses to arbitrate.

- Do laypeople sit on the panel? How many?

- How much is the filing fee? Is this fee refundable? Under what circumstances?

Binding decisions cannot be appealed

- Is the arbitration binding? Usually the decision of the arbitration panel is final and *cannot be appealed*.

- Does the bar publish a brochure describing the rules and procedures in your state?

Filing for Arbitration

The following step-by-step approach to arbitrating a disputed fee is a streamlined version of pioneer systems developed in Washington State and Massachusetts about 10 years ago. These systems were based on the fairly complex pattern for arbitration used by the American Arbitration Association. Keep in mind that the steps vary for each area.

State-level
arbitration
may be better

- Find out if your state or locality has fee arbitration (see Appendix III). A local board is more likely to be acquainted with and sympathetic to your lawyer, so a state board is probably preferable. If your area does not offer fee arbitration, your only recourse is to take the disputed fee to court (see Chapter 9). Ask about filing fees.

- Fill out a request for arbitration. Include a brief but complete description of your complaint and copies of any documentation you have to prove your case.

- The fee arbitration board will ask your lawyer to agree to arbitrate and explain the rules to both of you.

Case may be
decided without a
hearing

- The board may decide your case based solely on the information you and your lawyer provided, particularly if little money is involved.

- If a decision was not made based on the papers filed, you will be given a hearing time and place and told the names of the arbitrators, usually three.

- Either you or your lawyer can reject an arbitrator and ask for a substitute.

- Prepare for the hearing by organizing your evidence and preparing arguments. Bring copies of your fee agreement, bills, letters and any other documents that relate to fees.

- Rules for hearings differ from state to state. Usually, the hearing is conducted by one to three local lawyers and lay panelists selected at random from lists of volunteers. It is usually held at a mutually convenient place.

- The hearings tend to be informal and brief. Rules of evidence do not apply. Either side may be represented by an attorney, but need not be.

- The panel will make a decision and notify you in writing. Some states require a written decision stating the reasons for the decision. If the arbitration is binding, it is enforceable in court and you have no right to appeal. If the arbitration is not binding, you may pursue your case in court.

Attorney Discipline

State bar associations, the official agencies that license lawyers, have disciplinary or grievance committees charged with making sure only honest, competent lawyers are licensed. Each state has a "Code of Professional Responsibility" or "Model Rules of Professional Conduct" which spells out the rules lawyers must work by. This is usually based on a model written by the American Bar Association. The rules are enforced by the highest court of the state, either directly or by supervising state bar enforcement and providing judicial oversight and interpretation of ethical standards.

Conduct rules enforced by highest state court

You can get a copy of the Code of Professional Responsibility for your state from a public law library or the state bar association. In general, most states can discipline attorneys found guilty of:

- Acts of moral turpitude — felonies or misdemeanors involving malice or lying.
- Dishonesty, fraud or misrepresentation.
- Mixing a client's money with the attorney's own funds ("comingling") or stealing from a client.

- Accepting employment when the work may be affected by a personal, financial or business interest.
- Failure to act competently.

You get no money, even if complaint is valid

If you complain about a lawyer to your state or local disciplinary committee, the lawyer can be disciplined but *you will not receive any compensation from the bar through this procedure, even if your complaint is determined to be valid.*

Only about 5 percent of all complaints result in discipline. There are four basic types of discipline, although not every state uses all four.

Private Reprimand. Only you, the panel and the disciplined lawyer are told what happened. The lawyer is confidentially told, in effect, to "go and sin no more." This occurs in about 2.5 percent of all cases.

Public Reprimand. A "public" notice of the reprimand is published, usually in the state bar journal or newspaper distributed to lawyers licensed in the state. The lawyer may be embarrassed among colleagues, but the information will only reach the limited readership of the journal. About 1.5 percent of all cases.

Suspension. A suspension can range from a few days to several years. During this time, the lawyer is not licensed to practice law in that state. Less than 1 percent of all cases.

Disbarment. This is the severest penalty available. It is used only when an attorney is found guilty of repeated misconduct, gross misconduct, or is convicted of a felony. An attorney who is disbarred may not practice law in that state. Another state may allow the attorney to practice, however. Less than one fifth of 1 percent of all cases.

Most disciplinary programs are burdened with major flaws:

- In about half the states, the reviewing panels are composed entirely of lawyers.

*Proceedings
usually
kept secret*

- In most states, the proceedings are secret, and even the decisions are kept secret unless they result in a public reprimand, suspension or disbarment.

- If no public action is taken, even the complaining client is sworn to secrecy.

- Usually, the attorney can appeal the decision, but not the client.

- The committees' powers are limited to the punishments at their disposal and by the lack of clarity in the wording of the standards they enforce.

- Investigative resources are limited and long delays are common. It can take years to handle a case. In California, for example, four-year delays are routine.

- Some grievance committees seem to limit their attention to complaints against attorneys who are not associated with large, prestige law firms.

*Some states
outlaw
retaliation suits
by lawyers*

Many people considering a grievance complaint against their lawyer are worried that the lawyer will sue them for defamation. Such retaliation suits have been made illegal in some states, and where they are not illegal the court will often recognize their intent and take it into consideration. The main reason for filing such a suit is to discourage you from pursuing your complaint. If this happens to you, contact the disciplinary committee and ask what your rights are.

Why Complain?

Complaints bring pressure for reforms

Because filing a grievance seldom results in discipline and never brings the client any monetary relief, HALT is often asked why anyone should bother filing a complaint. One answer is that, if injured clients don't complain, statistics like those already cited in this chapter would not be available for use in challenging the bar to provide adequate consumer protection. When states have reformed their lawyer-discipline systems, it is almost always a direct result of public exposure of clear cases of lawyer misconduct in which disciplinary committees failed to act adequately.

One example: in 1985, a four-year scandal in Connecticut culminated in sweeping legislative reforms. The reforms were prompted by the jailing of a state representative for protesting the local disciplinary committee's failure to act adequately against three attorneys for their mishandling of a $38 million estate. The three attorneys and a judge had already been publicly criticized by another judge, a judicial ethics panel, and a legislative committee for stealing the elderly woman's property, invading her privacy and charging more than $500,000 in fees while wrestling over control of her estate.

Public outrage over jailing spurred changes in Connecticut

Even after media coverage of the case and the judge's resignation under threat of impeachment, the grievance committee delayed action for 15 months. It was only after a court ordered the committee to act that it recommended a private reprimand for one of the lawyers and public reprimands for the other two. When the legislator tried to protest the leniency, he was given a 10-day jail sentence for contempt of court. Public and legislative outrage over the jailing led to a major reform of Connecticut's grievance process, including nonlawyer involvement and public hearings.

In addition to supporting such reform efforts, complaining about your attorney's misconduct can also help assure that future clients of the same lawyer are spared your experience. Your case may be the fifth time your attorney's name has come up in such proceedings, establishing a pattern the committee can ignore. Also, pursuing your complaint can bolster claim that you fired your attorney for good cause and therefore shouldn't be required to pay fees. Finally your complaint could contribute to making the committee more accountable to consumers.

How To File a Complaint

Filing a complaint is easy, especially if you have been diligent about keeping good records, and it cost you nothing. You may hire an attorney to represent you, but most people don't because you get no money even if you "win." Follow these steps:

- Contact your state or local attorney grievance or disciplinary committee (see Appendix III and ask for a complaint form, if they have one and a copy of the rules.

- Fill out the forms or prepare a brief written summary of your complaint. If the complaint form does not give you adequate space to explain your side, attach additional sheets.

- Enclose copies of bills, letters, receipts, case documents and any other documentation that supports your claim.

- Keep a copy of your complaint and the originals of any attachments or enclosures.

The grievance committee will ask your lawyer for a response to your complaint and allow at least two weeks for that response. The committee may make its decision based solely on the information you and your lawyer provided, so it is important to present your case well when you file a complaint. It may well be your last chance to offer information.

Alternatively, you may be asked for further information or notified of a hearing time and place. Prepare for the hearing by:

- Organizing your evidence and arguments.
- Gathering copies of all relevant documents.
- Preparing a clear presentation using your written records to cite specific instances of misconduct.

Your presentation should be factual, not argumentative or based on impressions. Make every attempt to appear logical and careful.

Rules of evidence don't apply

Rules for hearings vary significantly from state to state. In general, the rules of evidence don't apply. Many states do not require the lawyer to attend the hearing. Some states do not allow you to ask the lawyer questions, but do allow the lawyer to question you. Some states don't even allow you to be present during the lawyer's presentation or to call on witnesses. Finally, either person can be represented by a lawyer, but need not be.

After the hearing, the panel will deliberate. In most places it is required to present its recommendation to the court or the bar association. This body then decides to approve, reject or modify the recommendation. Usually, however, the recommendation is approved without question. You will be sent a letter notifying you if discipline is to be imposed. In some states, you are sent a written decision that includes the panel's reasoning. This information is made public only if "public" discipline has been approved.

In some states, you are not allowed to appeal a decision that favors the lawyer but the lawyer can appeal an adverse decision. You are not allowed to offer evidence at this appeal hearing, but at least you may be able to attend, as appeals are usually public.

Chapter 9:

SUING A LAWYER

You may get an award AND attorney fees

If you sue your lawyer for malpractice and win, you can be awarded money and, sometimes, attorney fees. You can sue for malpractice whether or not you have filed a grievance or a claim with a client security fund. In some states, you must file your suit within two years of when the malpractice occurred; in others, this "statute of limitations" is four years.

You can win a malpractice suit even if you don't prove a violation of the disciplinary rules. In particular, carelessness or negligence may not be grounds for discipline but could well be grounds for a successful malpractice suit.

You must prove two cases in one—

The standard used to judge malpractice is whether the attorney used the skill, care and diligence of a lawyer of ordinary skill who takes similar cases in your area. A malpractice suit must jump some significant hurdles, however. In actuality, you have to prove two cases in one. First, you must prove that your attorney's conduct fell below the standard. Second, you must show you suffered a monetary loss as a result of the attorney's misconduct.

—that the lawyer made a serious mistake—

The fact you lost the case for which you hired the lawyer isn't enough; one side always "loses" — unless you settle out of court. Instead, you must prove that your lawyer was incompetent, negligent or dishonest. That is, you must prove the attorney made errors of fact or judgment or failed to meet deadlines or do specific research, or was dishonest in managing your property. The errors must have been worse than those of an average lawyer in your area. And you must prove

—that the error lost you money

that those errors caused you to lose money, to lose your right to sue or to lose the right to collect money or property that was due you.

To show your attorney failed to meet the standard, you often need testimony from other lawyers in the area who are willing to state under oath that your attorney's work was below the standard for the community. In many smaller communities it can be difficult if not impossible to find an attorney willing to represent you in a malpractice case, much less one willing to be a witness for your side. For that reason if no other, it's always best to try to negotiate a settlement with the attorney before filing a suit. In negotiation you may be able to convince the lawyer that bad public relations and the expense of defending against a malpractice suit are not worth it. Most attorneys carry malpractice insurance. Unfortunately, unless the lawyer has committed an obvious error, such as missing a deadline or blatant dishonesty, the lawyer will probably successfully argue that the error was one of judgment only.

Get more than one opinion   Before filing a malpractice action, it is a good idea to consult a few attorneys about your case. Things you want to ask about include:

- Whether you can find an objective attorney to take the case, how much the attorney will charge, and whether you will be able to work with a new attorney after your recent problems.

- Whether you can take the case yourself to small claims court (see below).

- The probable cost of the suit. A malpractice suit can be very expensive because you usually need expert witnesses and the attorney is likely to use every legal recourse in defending against the suit, especially costly delays.

- The amount you can expect to win and your chances of winning it.

Malpractice in Small Claims Court

You do not need a lawyer in small claims court, although most states don't forbid you to have one. The major limitation of this option is that you can only sue for between $500 and $2,500, depending on the rules in your state or local area. The advantages, however, are that small claims courts offer simplified procedures, informal rules and an inexpensive setting in which to "take your lawyer to court."

Simple rules, informal setting

HALT's *Citizens Legal Manual,* **Small Claims Court,** provides a step-by-step guide to bringing a case in small claims courts. It also lists the limitations on the amount you can sue for in each state.

CONCLUSION

This manual is about a business relationship between two people, an attorney and a client. It lists techniques for avoiding potential problems with the attorney and your options for redress if and when those problems arise. The message of the manual is simple: take care in hiring, be diligent in managing and participating in your case, keep organized written records, use thought in firing, and be willing to pursue options for redress.

Most people go to a lawyer for help in circumstances that are worrisome. It is hard for most people to be careful and logical in such situations, but as is emphasized throughout this manual, to be otherwise is to invite problems that will compound the trouble which took you to the lawyer's office in the first place.

This manual exposes some of the serious failings of the current system for monitoring and disciplining attorney misconduct. HALT lobbies for the reform of laws and procedures and for increased public involvement in the regulation of legal practitioners. Until such reforms are adopted, however, wise clients will make sure they are fully informed and involved. Only then will they increase their chances of being satisfied with the results of their lawyer's efforts and the resolution of their legal concern.

Appendix I:

EMPLOYMENT CONTRACTS

Many attorneys now offer a standard one-page retainer agreement for their clients to sign. The principal reason for this short-form contract is the fear that a longer contract will merely intimidate a potential client. This fear, plus the fact that the primary focus of the document is often the client's agreement to pay, makes these forms necessarily incomplete.

The following contract was designed to secure the rights and stipulate the responsibilities of both the attorney and client. It is also meant to serve as a discussion document by which the client may learn enough about a particular attorney's business practices to make an informed choice as a consumer of legal services.

Use of the following contract (or a modified version of it) is, of course, a decision to be made entirely by the client and attorney. However, HALT's research has shown that most disputes between clients and attorneys could have been avoided if the nature of their relationship had been made explicit at the outset. If your attorney refuses to sign or draft a document such as this, ask why. The anwers will tell you whether or not the attorney is the sort you want to employ.

The contract printed in full on the following pages is an agreement to employ an attorney on an hourly-fee basis. For contingent or fixed-fee arrangements, replace Section One—Attorney's Fees with the appropriate Section One (Contingent or Fixed) which follows the full contract.

CONTRACT TO EMPLOY ATTORNEY

_____ (referred to in this contract as Client) o
        (name)
_____ requests and authorizes _____
        (address)   *(name)*
referred to in this contract as Attorney) of _____ a
                                        (name of firm)
_____ to represent Client as (his/her) Attorney in
        (address)
fact and in law as related to

> SPECIFIC DESCRIPTION OF NATURE AND EXTENT OF CASE
> (e.g., "a divorce proceeding between X and Y for which Attorney
> will conduct negotiations and make court appearances which are
> necessary to securing separation, custody, property and dissolu-
> tion agreements, including a final decree, but not including an
> appeal")

and against all additional persons, firms, or corporations who may appear to
be related to this case.

SECTION ONE
Attorney's Fees

Compensation for Attorney's services shall be based on an hourly fee
arrangement.

(1) Client will pay Attorney the sum of _____ Dollars ($_____) per hour for
Attorney's time spent in research, writing, consultation, conference with
opposing parties, and other matters specifically related to the case described above.

(2) Attorney's additional charges, if any, for appearances in court are as
follows:

Routine appearances (e.g., motions for
   continuances) $_____ per _____

Simple motions (e.g., for temporary custody,
   discovery motions, etc.) $_____ per _____

Trials or hearings $_____ per _____

(3) If a junior partner, associate, or staff attorney within the Firm performs research or other services for the Client, the Client will pay for those services at the rate of _____ Dollars ($____) per hour. Any court appearance of junior member of the firm will be charged to the Client at a rate of _____ percent (____%) of the court appearance charges of the Attorney, as given in I(1) above.

(4) For all services performed by paralegals for the Client, the Client will pay for those services at the rate of _____ Dollars ($____) per hour.

(5) If Client is to be charged for secretarial services, Client will pay for those services at the rate of _____ Dollars ($____) per hour.

(6) Time charges will be computed and billed to the tenth of an hour.

(7) It is necessary to incur certain court costs in order to successfully complete this case. Client agrees to pay for all additional court costs at the following rates:

- ☐ Filing fees $_____per_____
- ☐ Deposition fees $_____per_____
- ☐ Fees for court reporter $_____per_____
- ☐ Charges for transcripts $_____per_____
- ☐ Subpoena fees $_____per_____
- ☐ Fees for expert witnesses $_____per_____

(8) Attorney estimates that these court costs will not exceed the sum of _____ Dollars ($____).

(9) Client also agrees to pay for any of the additional costs checked below at the following rates:

- ☐ Charges for local phone calls $_____per_____
- ☐ Charges for postage (e.g., registered mail) $_____per_____
- ☐ Long distance phone charges   ____% of STD. RATE
- ☐ Document search and file (including computer time) $_____per_____
- ☐ Special research or investigation (e.g., a private investigator) $_____per_____
- ☐ Travel $_____per_____
- ☐ Other: _____ $_____

(10) Attorney estimates additional costs listed in (9) above will not exceed the sum of _____ Dollars ($____).

(11) Attorney shall pay all personal and travel expenses incurred within the (county/city) of _____.

(12) The total estimated number of hours required for the completion of this case are as follows: _____ hours by Attorney; _____ hours by junior members of firm; and _____ hours by paralegals.

(13) Attorney estimates that the total cost of fees for the services of Attorney, junior members, and paralegals will not exceed the sum of _____ Dollars ($____).

(14) Client will not be liable for any additional costs or fees which exceed the estimates given in I(8), I(10) and I(13) unless Attorney notifies Client of the additional expenses required and receives permission of Client *before* incurring the additional expenses.

(15) (OPTIONAL) The total cost of completing this case shall not under any circumstances exceed the estimates given in I(8), I(10) and I(13) by a factor of _____ percent (____%). [NOTE: For certain cases, there may be several unknown factors at the outset — e.g., whether or not the opposing party will decide to litigate or settle. Therefore, it may be necessary for Attorney and Client to set spending limits which are conditional upon certain events. For example, both "If the case is settled without litigation, the total cost. . . ," and "If litigation is required to settle the case. . . ," may be necessary.]

SECTION TWO
Billing Agreement

(1) Client will not be billed for Attorney's time in the preparation or discussion of this employment contract or in discussions concerning disputes over billing. Secretarial time may be charged for the preparation of the original document and copies, the charge to be included in the estimate of additional costs.

(2) Client will pay a retainer of _____ Dollars ($____) and receive a signed receipt from the Attorney for said amount.

(3) Client will receive a statement with detailed itemization of the Attorney's, junior members' and paralegals' activities in the case; the amount of time involved, and the additional costs incurred. This statement will be sent to the Client on a monthly (or other _____) basis (and/or) per unit of expenditure (e.g., each time the bill increases by $250, an updated statement is to be sent). If per-unit billing is adopted, that unit will be _____ Dollars ($____).

(4) All costs and expenses are to be deducted, unless otherwise noted, from the retainer. The current balance of the client's retainer is to be plainly indicated in each itemized statement.

(5) The Attorney's fees (may/may not) be deducted from the retainer.

(6) The Client is to be notified in writing prior to the depletion of the retainer.

(7) Should the retainer exceed the total cost of completing the case, the remainder is to be returned in full to the Client.

(8) Should the cost of conducting the case exceed the retainer but not the estimate or agreed maximum, the Client agrees to reimburse the Attorney for the additional costs (and/but not) the Attorney's fees within _____ (____) days of receipt of an itemized statement.

(9) If the total cost exceeds the retainer but not the agreed maximum, payment for outstanding fees and costs upon completion of the case shall be by (a lump sum payment/payment in full within thirty (30) days of submission of a properly itemized statement/monthly payments of _____ _____ Dollars ($_____)).

(10) Attorney shall receive no other compensation in any manner or form than that provided for expressly by this agreement.

SECTION THREE
Attorney's Rights and Responsibilities

(1) This contract represents earnest compliance with Ethical Consideration of the American Bar Association's Code of Professional Responsibility. Attorney consents to be bound by all Canons, Ethical Considerations and Disciplinary Rules of the ABA Code as amended June, 1983.

(2) Violation of any provision within the ABA Code or any agreement within this contract of employment shall be grounds for dismissal of the Attorney.

(3) As mandated by the ABA Code, Attorney shall regularly inform Client of progress, if any, in Client's case. This shall include copies of pleadings, briefs, memoranda and relevant correspondence as the case progresses.

(4) Attorney shall freely and frankly discuss the strategy and progress of the case with Client upon request. Attorney must consult and seek permission of Client before taking any action which may significantly affect the outcome or cost of the proceedings.

(5) Attorney may not under any circumstances agree to settle a case without the prior consent of Client.

(6) Withdrawal from representation by Attorney is mandatory upon discharge by Client.

SECTION FOUR
Client's Rights and Responsibilities

1) Client agrees to disclose truthfully all relevant information to Attorney upon request.

2) Client will make (himself/herself) and any documents, persons or things under the Client's control available to Attorney at reasonable times and places for such conferences, inspections, discussions and legal proceedings as may be necessary from time to time.

3) Client will promptly notify Attorney of any change in the Client's address or phone number.

4) In an effort to increase client participation and to reduce costs, Client will, at the direction of the Attorney, perform these tasks:

(E.G., LOCATING EVIDENCE, CONTACTING WITNESSES, FILING DOCUMENTS WITH COURT CLERK, ETC. SEE CHAPTER 1.)

(5) Failure of Client to seek counsel of Attorney before taking any action which may affect the course or resolution of the case represents sufficient grounds for Attorney withdrawal from employment.
(6) Attorney may not withdraw from employment unless (i) the Client receives fourteen (14) days notice prior to withdrawal, (ii) trial is not scheduled within 30 days, (iii) withdrawal will not significantly affect the outcome of imminent proceedings, and (iv) competent counsel may be obtained readily elsewhere by Client.
(7) In the event of withdrawal, Attorney will withdraw in writing and include reasons for withdrawing.
(8) Attorney may not condition completion of representation of Client upon payment of estimated or actual fee under any terms other than those stipulated within this contract.
(9) All documents presented by Client to Attorney remain the exclusive property of Client and must be returned upon demand. Attorney expressly relinquishes all general, possessory or retaining liens known to the common or statutory law.

SECTION FIVE
Disputes

(1) Attorney and Client recognize the benefits of maintaining a harmonious working relationship. Both agree to discuss openly any cause of dissatisfaction and to seek reconciliation. Client will not be billed for this discussion.
(2) Should either party believe itself to be seriously wronged or believe that the terms of this contract have been substantially violated, resolution shall be sought through binding arbitration by a third party mutually agreed to by both Attorney and Client.

SECTION SIX
Disclaimer of Warranty

No warranties have been made by Attorney with respect to the successful termination of this case. All expressions made by Attorney about the possible outcome of the case are matters of Attorney's opinion only.

SECTION SEVEN
Power of Attorney

Client grants a power of attorney to Attorney in order that Attorney may execute all documents relevant to the handling of this case, including pleadings, verifications, dismissals, orders and all other documents that Client could otherwise properly execute.

SECTION EIGHT
Notice

Any notice required under this agreement shall be in writing and shall be deemed to have been duly served if delivered in person, or if delivered at or sent by first class mail to the business address of the person for whom it is intended, as specified in this agreement.

SECTION NINE
Law To Govern Contract

The laws of the State of _____ shall govern the construction and interpretation of this agreement.

SECTION TEN

This contract is valid only with regard to the case described above. An appeal of this case to a higher court, or retrial before a similar court will require a separate employment contract.

This contract has been read, understood, signed and attested on this day _____, 19__, by the undersigned.

ATTORNEY(S)_____   CLIENT(S)_____

_____   _____

_____   _____

                               WITNESS_____

70

For A Contingent Fee Arrangement:

SECTION ONE
Attorney's Fees

Compensation for Attorney's services shall be based on a contingent fee arrangement.

(1) The contingent fee shall be based on a percentage of the actual recovery *after* all expenses indicated in I(3) and (5) below have been deducted

(2) The contingent fee rate will be _____ percent (_____%).

(OR)

    a. _____ percent (_____%) of the first _____ Dollars ($_____) of the award.

    b. _____ percent (_____%) of the next _____ Dollars ($_____) of the award.

    c. _____ percent (_____%) of the award that exceeds _____ Dollars ($_____).

(3) It is necessary to incur certain court costs in order to complete this case successfully. Client agrees to pay for all additional court costs at the following rates:

☐ Filing fees	$_____ per_____
☐ Deposition fees	$_____ per_____
☐ Fees for court reporter	$_____ per_____
☐ Charges for transcripts	$_____ per_____
☐ Subpoena fees	$_____ per_____
☐ Fees for expert witnesses	$_____ per_____

(4) Attorney estimates that these court costs will not exceed the sum of _____Dollars ($_____).

(5) Client also agrees to pay for any of the additional costs checked below at the following rates:

☐ Charges for local phone calls	$_____ per_____
☐ Charges for postage (e.g., registered mail)	$_____ per_____
☐ Long distance phone charges	_____% of STD. RATE
☐ Document search and file (including computer time)	$_____ per_____
☐ Special research or investigation (e.g., a private investigator)	$_____ per_____
☐ Travel	$_____ per_____
☐ Other:_____	$_____

71

6) Attorney estimates additional costs listed in (5) above will not exceed the sum of _____ Dollars ($_____).
7) Attorney shall pay all personal and travel expenses incurred within the (county/city) of _____.
8) The total estimated additional costs required for the completion of this case are $_____. If the case is settled before a decision of the court, these additional costs will be reduced accordingly.
9) Client may be requested to advance in part or in full the funds required to meet these costs. If so, this pre-payment is designated as the 'retainer' in Section Two (below).
10) Client will not be liable for any additional costs which exceed the estimate given in I(8) unless Attorney notifies Client of the additional expenses required and receives permission of Client *before* incurring the additional expenses.
11) (OPTIONAL) The total additional costs and expenses incurred in completing this case shall not under any circumstances exceed the estimate given in I(8) by a factor of 20%.
12) If the case is lost, Client is liable only for the costs incurred, within the limits determined by I(8) and I(11) (if applicable). Client is also liable for opponent's costs, should the court so decide.
13) The decision to appeal against the verdict of the court is the exclusive right of Client.
14) Attorney is (given/denied) a special or charging lien on the claim or cause of action, on any sum recovered by way of settlement, and on any judgment that may be recovered, for the sum mentioned above as his fee. That is, Client (is/is not) free to use any portion of the recovery for personal purposes until Attorney's fee is paid.
15) Costs and expenses incurred by Attorney in advancing Client's cause are to be borne by Client. All costs which are not covered by funds advanced by Client to Attorney will be (paid by Client in periodic billings/ advanced by Attorney, with reimbursement to be made from the gross proceeds of any recovery, which reimbursements shall be in addition to the percentage fee).
16) If Client settles the claim without consent of Attorney, Client will pay Attorney a fee computed in accordance with the terms of this agreement and based on the final recovery by Client in the settlement, and Client will reimburse Attorney for all advances made for costs and other expenses.

For a Fixed Fee Arrangement:

SECTION ONE
Attorney's Fees

Compensation of Attorney's services shall be based on a fixed fee arrange-ment.

(1) Client will pay Attorney the sum of _____ Dollars ($_____) as full reimbursement for the completion of all services required to conclude and resolve all aspects of the case described above.

(2) The fixed fee amount given in I(1) above does not include any of the additional costs checked below. Client agrees to pay for all additional court costs at the following rates:

☐ Filing fees $_____per_____
☐ Deposition fees $_____per_____
☐ Fees for court reporter $_____per_____
☐ Charges for transcripts $_____per_____
☐ Subpoena fees $_____per_____
☐ Fees for expert witnesses $_____per_____

(3) Attorney estimates that these court costs will not exceed the sum of _____ Dollars ($_____).

(4) Client also agrees to pay for any of the additional costs checked below at the following rates:

☐ Charges for local phone calls $_____per_____
☐ Charges for postage (e.g., registered mail) $_____per_____
☐ Long distance phone charges   _____% of STD. RATE
☐ Document search and file (including
    computer time $_____per_____
☐ Special research or investigation (e.g., a
    private investigator) $_____per_____
☐ Travel $_____per_____
☐ Other:_____ $_____

(5) Attorney estimates additional costs listed in (4) above will not exceed the sum of _____Dollars ($_____).

(6) Attorney shall pay all personal and travel expenses incurred within the county/city) of _____.

(7) Time charges for any of the additional costs checked above will be computed and billed to the tenth of an hour.

(8) Client will not be liable for any additional costs which exceed the estimates given in I(3) and I(5) unless Attorney notifies Client of the additional expense required and receives permission of Client *before* incurring the additional costs.

(9) (OPTIONAL) The total cost of completing this case shall not under any circumstances exceed the sum of _____ Dollars ($_____).

CASE FLOW CHART AND GLOSSARY

HOW A CASE MOVES THROUGH THE COURTS

PLEADING STAGE

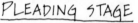

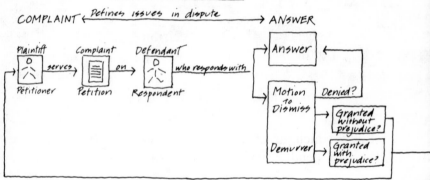

COMPLAINT → Defines issues in dispute → ANSWER

Plaintiff / Petitioner — serves — Complaint / Petition — on — Defendant / Respondent — who responds with →

- Answer ←
- Motion to Dismiss — Denied? → Granted without prejudice?
- Demurrer → Granted with prejudice?

PRE-TRIAL STAGE

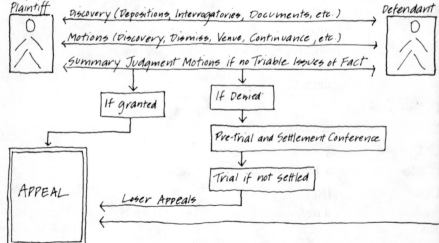

Plaintiff — Defendant

Discovery (Depositions, Interrogatories, Documents, etc.)

Motions (Discovery, Dismiss, Venue, Continuance, etc.)

Summary Judgment Motions if no Triable Issues of Fact

If granted → APPEAL

If Denied → Pre-trial and Settlement Conference → Trial if not settled

Loser Appeals → APPEAL

Reprinted by permission of Nolo Press. © 1984

AFFIDAVIT
A written statement of fact voluntarily signed and sworn to before a person having authority to administer an oath.

ANSWER
The *defendant's* formal statement of defense against the *plaintiff's* claim in a lawsuit. The answer addresses the truth or falsity of claims made in the plaintiff's *complaint* and can include a counter-complaint.

APPEAL
A request that a higher court review the decision of a lower court in order to correct errors in the application of law or procedure.

APPELLANT
A person who initiates an *appeal*.

ATTACHMENT
The method by which property, real or personal, is legally taken by a creditor and held pending the outcome of a lawsuit over a debt.

BRIEF
A written statement prepared by one side in a lawsuit to explain to a judge the essential facts of a case and the applicable law.

COMPLAINT
The paper which officially initiates a lawsuit. It includes, among other things, a statement of the facts and the wrong or harm done to the complaining side (*plaintiff*) by the other side (*defendant*), a request for help from the court and an explanation of why the court has the power to do what the complaining side wants.

CONTEMPT
Willful disobedience of a judge's command or an official court order.

CONTINUANCE
Postponement of a legal proceeding to a later date.

COUNTERCLAIM
A claim made by a *defendant* in a civil lawsuit that, in effect, sues the *plaintiff*.

Italicized words are defined in other entries in this glossary.

CROSSCLAIM
A claim litigated by co-defendants or co-plaintiffs against each other and not against persons on the opposite side of the litigation.

DEFAULT JUDGMENT
A decision in favor of the *plaintiff* because the *defendant* failed to file pleadings in response to the plaintiff's complaint within the time required by law.

DEFENDANT
The person against whom a legal action is taken.

DEPOSITION
The out-of-court process of taking a witness' sworn testimony. This is usually done by a lawyer, with a lawyer from the other side afforded a chance to attend or participate. The purpose is to narrow the issues and disclose relevant information so that each side can evaluate its case before going to trial and decide whether to pursue the claim or settle out of court.

DISCOVERY
The formal and informal exchange of information between sides in a lawsuit before going to trial. Two types of discovery are *interrogatories* and *depositions*.

GARNISHMENT
A legal proceeding whereby a debtor's wages, property, money or credits are taken to satisfy payment of a debt or judgment.

INJUNCTION
A judge's order to do or to refrain from doing a specified thing. For example, a court might issue an injunction ordering a manufacturing company to stop dumping toxic wastes into a river.

INTERROGATORIES
Written questions which require written response under oath by a party in a lawsuit.

JUDGMENT
The final decision announced or written by a judge about the rights and claims of each side in a lawsuit.

LIEN
A legal claim to hold or sell property as security for a debt.

MOTION
A request that a judge take some specific action. For example, a motion to dismiss is a request that the judge throw a case out of court.

MOTION TO ENLARGE
A request for more time than is allowed by court rules.

ORDER
A written command or direction by a judge or court clerk. Orders may outline a decision of the court, direct or forbid an action, or be the final decision of the court.

PLAINTIFF
A person who starts a lawsuit against another person.

PLEADING
The process of making formal written statements of the claims and defenses of each side in a lawsuit.

PRETRIAL CONFERENCE
A meeting of lawyers and judges, sometimes including the parties themselves, to narrow the issues in a lawsuit, agree on what will be presented at the trial, and make a final effort to settle the case without trial.

PROTECTIVE ORDER
1. A court order that temporarily allows one side to hold back from showing the other side documents or other materials that were properly requested.
2. Any court order protecting a person from harassment, service of process or similiar problems.

RESPONDENT
1. The person against whom a motion is filed. 2. The person against whom an appeal is taken.

RULING
A judge's decision on a legal question raised during a trial.

SERVICE
The delivery of a legal paper by an officially authorized person in a way that meets all formal requirements stated by the applicable laws. It is used to officially notify a person of a lawsuit or other legal action against them.

SETTLEMENT
An agreement about the disposition of a lawsuit, including payment of debts, costs, etc.

SUBPOENA
A notice issued by a court to compel the appearance of a witness or submission of documents or other evidence at a judicial hearing; disobedience may be punishable as contempt of court.

SUMMONS
1. A notice delivered by a sheriff or other authorized person informing you that you are being sued. It tells you to show up in court at a certain time to tell your side of the story or risk losing the suit because of your absence (*default judgment*). 2. A notice delivered by a sheriff or other authorized person informing you to appear before a grand jury.

SUMMARY JUDGMENT
A court's final decision based on the facts but issued before the conclusion of a full trial.

TEMPORARY RESTRAINING ORDER
A judge's order forbidding certain actions before a full hearing can be held on the facts of the case involved. Often referred to as a T.R.O.

TESTIMONY
Oral or written evidence in the form of questions and answers given under oath.

THIRD PARTY CLAIM
An action by the *defendant* that brings a third party into a lawsuit.

TRANSCRIPT
The official typed copy of the record of testimony taken under oath during the trial.

Appendix III
STATE PROGRAMS FOR RESOLVING COMPLAINTS

This appendix lists addresses and phone numbers for grievance committees, client security fund offices and fee arbitration programs for the 50 states, the District of Columbia, the Virgin Islands and Puerto Rico.

Where state offices handle the matter, that office is listed. If the issue is handled at a local office, that office is either listed or we suggest you contact the state office for a local referral.

All information is accurate as of July 1985. Data on grievance committees and client security fund offices were compiled by the American Bar Association and the fee arbitration program data were compiled by HALT. Because the names and addresses of state agencies may change at any time, you should verify the information with your state bar or the American Bar Association.

ALABAMA
Attorney Grievance
State Office:
 Center For Professional Responsibility
 1019 S. Perry St.
 Montgomery, AL 36104
 (205) 269-1514

Client Security Fund
 Alabama State Bar
 P.O. Box 671
 Montgomery, AL 36101
 (205) 269-1515

Fee Arbitration
 State bar refers cases to local fee arbitration where available.

 (Address, telephone same as Client Security Fund.)

ALASKA
Attorney Grievance
State Office:
 Disciplinary Administrator
 Alaska Bar Assn.
 P.O. Box 100279
 Anchorage, AK 99510
 (907) 272-7469

Client Security Fund
 (Address, telephone same as for Attorney Grievance.)

Fee Arbitration
 (Address, telephone same as for Attorney Grievance.)

ARIZONA
Attorney Grievance
State Office:
Chief Bar Counsel
State Bar of Arizona
363 N. First Ave.
Phoenix, AZ 85003
(602) 252-4804

Client Security Fund
(Address, telephone same as for Attorney
Grievance.)

Fee Arbitration
Complaints referred for local hearing.

State Bar of Arizona
234 N. Central Ave., Ste. 858
Phoenix, AZ 85004
(602) 252-4804

ARKANSAS
Attorney Grievance
State Office:
Committee on Professional Conduct
364 Prospect Bldg.
1501 N. University
Little Rock, AR 72207
(501) 664-8658

Client Security Fund
Client Security Fund Committee
Arkansas Supreme Court
Justice Bldg.
Little Rock, AR 72201
(501) 371-5614

Fee Arbitration
None.

CALIFORNIA
Attorney Grievance
Southern California:
Complaint Intake
State Bar of California
1230 W. Third St.
Los Angeles, CA 90017
(213) 482-8220

CALIFORNIA *(continued)*
Northern California:
Chief Trial Counsel
State Bar of California
555 Franklin St.
San Francisco, CA 94102
(415) 561-8200

Client Security Fund
Southern California Grievance
Committee district office handles all
cases.

(Address, telephone same as Southern
California Grievance Committee.)

Fee Arbitration
Northern California district office refers
complaints for local hearing.

Mandatory Fee Arbitration
(Address, telephone same as Northern
California Grievance Committee.)

COLORADO
Attorney Grievance
State Office:
Committee Counsel
Supreme Court
State of Colorado
190 E. 9th Ave., Ste. 440
Denver, CO 80203
(303) 832-3701

Client Security Fund
Colorado Bar Assn.
250 W. 14th Ave., Ste. 800
Denver, CO 80204
(303) 860-1112

Fee Arbitration
Complaints referred for local hearing.

Legal Fee Arbitration Committee
Colorado Bar Assn.
1900 Grant St., Ste. 950
Denver, CO 80203
(303) 860-1112

CONNECTICUT
Attorney Grievance
State Office:
Statewide Grievance Committee
7 Grand St.
P.O. Box 6225, Station A
Hartford, CT 06106
(203) 247-6264

District Offices:
(All district offices are scheduled to be
abolished and all complaints handled by
the state committee beginning July,
1986.)

District Grievance Committee
13 First Ave.
Waterbury, CT 06702
(203) 757-0311

District Grievance Committee
1016 Broad St.
Bridgeport, CT 06604
(203) 335-0108

District Grievance Committee
62 LaSalle Rd.
West Hartford, CT 06107
(203) 521-7500

District Grievance Committee
302 Captain's Walk
New London, CT 06320
(203) 443-8396

District Grievance Committe
129 Church St.
New Haven, CT 06510
(203) 777-7341

Client Security Fund
Connecticut Bar Assn.
101 Corporate Pl.
Rocky Hill, CT 06067
(203) 721-0025

Fee Arbitration
Complaints referred for local hearing.

Legal Fee Arbitration Committee
(Address, telephone same as Client
Security Fund.)

DELAWARE
Attorney Grievance
State Office:
Board on Professional Responsibility of
the Supreme Court
12th and Market Sts.
P.O. Box 1347
Wilmington, DE 19899
(302) 658-9200

Client Security Fund
Delaware State Bar Assn.
Carvel State Office Bldg.
820 N. French St.
Wilmington, DE 19801
(302) 658-5278

Fee Arbitration
Complaints referred for local hearing.

Fee Dispute Conciliation and Mediation
Committee
(Address, telephone same as Client
Security Fund.)

DISTRICT OF COLUMBIA
Attorney Grievance
District Office:
Office of Bar Counsel
Bldg. A, Rm. 127
515 5th St., N.W.
Washington, D.C. 20001
(202) 638-1501

Client Security Fund
District of Columbia Bar
1707 L St., N.W., 6th Fl.
Washington, D.C. 20036
(202) 331-3883

Fee Arbitration
(Address, telephone same as Client
Security Fund.)

FLORIDA
Attorney Grievance
State Office:
Staff Counsel
Florida Bar
Florida Bar Center
Tallahassee, FL 32301
(904) 222-5286

Client Security Fund
Client Security Fund Committee
(Address, telephone same as for
Attorney Grievance.)

Fee Arbitration
State bar refers cases to local fee
arbitration where available.

(Address, telephone same as for
Attorney Grievance.)

GEORGIA
Attorney Grievance
State Office:
General Counsel
State Bar of Georgia
Georgia Justice Center
84 Peachtree St., 11th Fl.
Atlanta, GA 30303
(404) 522-6255

Client Security Fund
(Address, telephone same as for Attorney
Grievance.)

Fee Arbitration
Complaints referred for local hearing.

Committee on Arbitration of Fee
Disputes
(Address, telephone same as for
Attorney Grievance.)

HAWAII
Attorney Grievance
State Office:
Office of Disciplinary Counsel
Supreme Court of Hawaii
1164 Bishop St., Ste. 600
Honolulu, HI 96813
(808) 521-4591

HAWAII *(continued)*
Client Security Fund
Hawaii State Bar Assn.
P.O. Box 26
Honolulu, HI 96810
(808) 537-1868

Fee Arbitration
Complaints referred for local hearing.

Committee for the Mediation/Arbitration
of Fee Disputes
(Address, telephone same as Client
Security Fund.)

IDAHO
Attorney Grievance
State Office:
Idaho State Bar Counsel
P.O. Box 895
204 W. State St.
Boise, ID 83701
(208) 342-8958

Client Security Fund
(Address, telephone same as for Attorney
Grievance.)

Fee Arbitration
Complaints referred for local hearing.

(Address, telephone same as for
Attorney Grievance.)

ILLINOIS
Attorney Grievance
Chicago and Northern Illinois:
Attorney Disciplinary Commission of
the Supreme Court
203 N. Wabash Ave., Ste. 1900
Chicago, IL 60601
(312) 346-0690

Central and Southern Illinois:
Attorney Disciplinary Commission of
the Supreme Court
One N. Old Capitol Plaza, Ste. 330
Springfield, IL 62701
(217) 522-6838
(800) 252-8048 (In Illinois)

ILLINOIS *(continued)*
Client Security Fund
 Clients' Security Fund
 Illinois Bar Center
 Springfield, IL 62701
 (217) 525-1760

Fee Arbitration
 Complaints referred for local hearing.

 Committee on Voluntary Fee Arbitration
 (Address same as Client Security Fund.)

INDIANA
Attorney Grievance
State Office:
 Disciplinary Commission of the
   Supreme Court
 I.S.T.A. Bldg., Rm. 814
 150 W. Market St.
 Indianapolis, IN 46204
 (317) 232-1807

Client Security Fund
 Clients' Financial Assistance Fund
   Committee
 Indiana State Bar Assn.
 230 E. Ohio St., 6th Fl.
 Indianapolis, IN 46204
 (317) 639-5465

Fee Arbitration
 State bar refers cases to local fee
 arbitration where available.
 (Address, telephone same as Client
 Security Fund.)

IOWA
Attorney Grievance
State Office:
 Iowa State Bar Assn.
 1101 Fleming Bldg.
 Des Moines, IA 50309
 (515) 243-3179

Client Security Fund
 Supreme Court Administrator
 State Capitol
 E. Fifth and Locust Sts.
 Des Moines, IA 50319
 (515) 281-3718

IOWA *(continued)*
Fee Arbitration
 Complaints referred for local hearing.

 Ethics Administrator
 (Address, telephone same as for
 Attorney Grievance.)

KANSAS
Attorney Grievance
State Office:
 Disciplinary Administrator
 Kansas Judicial Center, Rm. 278
 301 W. 10th St.
 Topeka, KS 66612
 (913) 296-2486

Client Security Fund
 Kansas Bar Assn.
 1200 Harrison St.
 P.O. Box 1037
 Topeka, KS 66061
 (913) 234-5696

Fee Arbitration
 No state or local bar-sponsored fee
 arbitration program. A private
 corporation in Topeka will arbitrate fee
 disputes for local residents.

 Dispute Alternate Resolution Center
 3600 Burlingame Rd., Ste. 1A
 Topeka, KS 66611
 (913) 357-7050

KENTUCKY
Attorney Grievance
State Office:
 Kentucky Bar Assn.
 W. Main at Kentucky River
 Frankfort, KY 40601
 (502) 564-3795

Client Security Fund
 (Address, telephone same as for Attorney
 Grievance.)

Fee Arbitration
 Complaints referred for local hearing.

 (Address, telephone same as for
 Attorney Grievance.)

LOUISIANA
Attorney Grievance
State Office:
Executive Counsel
Louisiana State Bar Assn.
210 O'Keefe Ave., Ste. 600
New Orleans, LA 70112
(504) 566-1600

Client Security Fund
(Address, telephone same as for Attorney Grievance.)

Fee Arbitration
None.

MAINE
Attorney Grievance
State Office:
Grievance Commission
Board of Overseers of the Bar
P.O. Box 1820
Augusta, ME 04330
(207) 623-1121

Client Security Fund
State Bar Executive
124 State St.
P.O. Box 788
Augusta, ME 04330
(207) 622-7523

Fee Arbitration
Complaints referred for local hearing.

Board of Overseers of the Bar
(Address, telephone same as for Attorney Grievance.)

MARYLAND
Attorney Grievance
State Office:
Office of the Bar Counsel
Attorney Grievance Commission
District Court Bldg., 4th Fl.
580 Taylor Ave.
Annapolis, MD 21401
(301) 269-2791

MARYLAND *(continued)*
Client Security Fund
Maryland State Bar Assn.
207 E. Redwood St., Ste. 905
Baltimore, MD 21202
(301) 685-7878

Fee Arbitration
Complaints referred for local hearing.

Committee on Resolution of Fee
Disputes
(Address same as Client Security Fund.)
(301) 766-0090

MASSACHUSETTS
Attorney Grievance
State Office:
Bar Counsel
Board of Bar Overseers of the Supreme
  Judicial Court
11 Beacon St.
Boston, MA 02108
(617) 720-0700

Client Security Fund
Client Security Board
(Address, telephone same as for
Attorney Grievance.)

Fee Arbitration
Complaints referred for local hearing.

Fee Arbitration Board
Massachusetts Bar Assn.
20 West St.
Boston, MA 02111
(617) 542-3602

MICHIGAN
Attorney Grievance
State Office:
Grievance Administrator
Attorney Grievance Commission
243 W. Congress
Detroit, MI 48226
(313) 961-6585

MICHIGAN *(continued)*
Client Security Fund
State Bar of Michigan
306 Townsend St.
Lansing, MI 48933
(517) 372-9030

Fee Arbitration
Complaints referred for local hearing.

(Address, telephone same as for
Attorney Grievance.)

MINNESOTA
Attorney Grievance
State Office:
Lawyers Professional Responsibility
   Board
444 Lafayette Rd., 4th Fl.
Saint Paul, MN 55101
(612) 296-3952

Client Security Fund
Minnesota Bar Assn.
430 Marquette Ave., Ste. 403
Minneapolis, MN 55401
(612) 333-1183

Fee Arbitration
State bar refers cases to local fee
arbitration where available.

(Address, telephone same as Client
Security Fund.)

MISSISSIPPI
Attorney Grievance
State Office:
General Counsel
Mississippi State Bar
P.O. Box 2168
Jackson, MS 39225
(601) 948-4471

Client Security Fund
(Address, telephone same as for Attorney
Grievance.)

MISSISSIPPI *(continued)*
Fee Arbitration
Complaints referred for local hearing.
(Address, telephone same as for Attorney
Grievance.)

MISSOURI
Attorney Grievance
State Office:
Advisory Committee
Missouri Bar Administration
P.O. Box 349
Sedalia, MO 65301
(816) 826-7890

Client Security Fund
Missouri Bar
P.O. Box 119
Jefferson City, MO 65102
(314) 635-4128

Fee Arbitration
State bar refers cases to local fee
arbitration where available.

(Address, telephone same as for
Attorney Grievance.)

MONTANA
Attorney Grievance
State Office:
Commission on Practice of the Supreme
   Court
Box 523
Livingston, MT 59047
(406) 222-2023

Client Security Fund
State Bar of Montana
P.O. Box 4669
Helena, MT 59604
(406) 442-7660

Fee Arbitration
State bar refers cases to local fee
arbitration where available.

(Address, telephone same as Client
Security Fund.)

NEBRASKA
Attorney Grievance
State Office:
Counsel for Discipline
Nebraska State Bar Assn.
1019 American Charter Center
206 S. 13th St.
Lincoln, NE 68508
(402) 475-7091

Client Security Fund
(Address, telephone same as for Attorney Grievance.)

Fee Arbitration
None.

NEVADA
Attorney Grievance
State Office:
Bar Counsel
State Bar of Nevada
601 E. Bridger
Las Vegas, NV 89101
(702) 329-4100

Client Security Fund
State Bar of Nevada
834 Willow St.
Reno, NV 89502
(702) 329-4100

Fee Arbitration
Complaints handled at either of the above offices.

NEW HAMPSHIRE
Attorney Grievance
State Office:
Professional Conduct Committee
New Hampshire Supreme Court
18 N. Main St., Ste. 205
Concord, NH 03301
(603) 224-5828

Client Security Fund
Clients' Indemnity Fund
New Hampshire Bar Assn.
18 Centre St.
Concord, NH 03301
(603) 224-6942

NEW HAMPSHIRE *(continued)*
Fee Arbitration
Complaints referred for local hearing.

Fee Dispute Resolution Committee
(Address, telephone same as Client Security Fund.)

NEW JERSEY
Attorney Grievance
State Office:
Office of Attorney Ethics
Supreme Court of New Jersey
Richard J. Hughes Justice Complex
Trenton, NJ 08625
(609) 292-7777

Client Security Fund
Administrative Office of the Courts
(Address same as for Attorney Grievance.)
(609) 292-8009

Fee Arbitration
Complaints referred for local hearing.

(Address same as for Attorney Grievance.)
(609) 292-8750

NEW MEXICO
Attorney Grievance
State Office:
Disciplinary Board
Scandia Savings Bldg., Ste. 712
Gold and Fourth Sts.
Albuquerque, NM 87102
(505) 842-5781

Client Security Fund
New Mexico State Bar
P.O. Box 25883
Albuquerque, NM 87125
(505) 842-6132

Fee Arbitration
Complaints referred for local hearing.

(Address, telephone same as Client Security Fund.)

NEW YORK
Attorney Grievance
Bronx County:
Departmental Disciplinary Committee
41 Madison Ave., 39th Fl.
New York, NY 10010
(212) 685-1000

Kings, Queens, Richmond Counties:
State of New York Grievance
    Committee
Municipal Bldg., 12th Fl.
210 Joralemon St.
Brooklyn, NY 11201
(212) 624-7851

Nassau, Suffolk Counties:
Joint Bar Assn. Grievance Committee
900 Ellison Ave.
Westbury, NY 11590
(516) 832-8585

Other District Offices:
District Grievance Committee
200 Bloomingdale Rd.
White Plains, NY 10605
(914) 949-4540

Committee on Professional Standards
P.O. Box 7013
Capitol Station Annex
Albany, NY 12225
(518) 474-8816

5th District Grievance Committee
472 S. Salina St., Rm. 310
Syracuse, NY 13202
(315) 471-1835

7th District Grievance Committee
19 W. Main, Rm. 1002
Rochester, NY 14614
(716) 546-8340

Grievance Committee
Ellicott Square Bldg., Rm. 1036
Buffalo, NY 14203
(716) 855-1191

NEW YORK *(continued)*
Client Security Fund
Clients Security Fund
55 Elk St.
Albany, NY 12224
(518) 474-8438

Fee Arbitration
County bar joint committee refers all state
complaints for local hearings.

Joint Committee on Fee Disputes and
    Conciliation
New York County Lawyers' Assn.
14 Vesey St.
New York, NY 10007
(212) 267-6646

NORTH CAROLINA
Attorney Grievance
State Office:
Counsel
North Carolina State Bar
208 Fayetteville St. Mall
P.O. Box 25908
Raleigh, NC 27611
(919) 828-4620

Client Security Fund
North Carolina State Bar
P.O. Box 25850
Raleigh, NC 27611
(919) 828-4620

Fee Arbitration
None.

NORTH DAKOTA
Attorney Grievance
State Office:
Disciplinary Counsel
Disciplinary Board of the Supreme
    Court
P.O. Box 2297
Bismarck, ND 58502
(701) 224-3348

NORTH DAKOTA (continued)
Client Security Fund
State Bar of North Dakota
P.O. Box 2136
Bismarck, ND 58502
(701) 255-1404

Fee Arbitration
Complaints referred for local hearing.

(Address, telephone same as Client
Security Fund.)

OHIO
Attorney Grievance
State Office:
Office of Disciplinary Counsel of the
    Supreme Court
175 S. Third St., Rm. 280
Columbus, OH 43215
(614) 461-0256

Summit County:
Akron Bar Assn.
90 S. High St.
Akron, OH 44308
(216) 253-5007

Hamilton County:
Cincinnati Bar Assn.
26 E. 6th St., Ste. 400
Cincinnati, OH 45202
(513) 381-8213

Cuyahoga County:
Bar Assn. of Greater Cleveland
Mall Bldg., 2nd. Fl.
118 Saint Clair Ave.
Cleveland, OH 44114
(216) 696-3525

Franklin County:
Columbus Bar Assn.
66 S. Third
Columbus, OH 43215
(614) 221-4112

Montgomery County:
Dayton Bar Assn.
1700 Hulman Bldg.
Dayton, OH 45402
(513) 222-7902

OHIO (continued)
Lucas County:
Toledo Bar Assn.
Commodore Perry Arcade
505 Jefferson
Toledo, OH 43604
(419) 242-9363

Client Security Fund
Ohio Supreme Court
30 E. Broad St.
Columbus, OH 43215
(614) 466-2653

Fee Arbitration
State bar refers cases to local fee
arbitration where available.

Ohio State Bar Assn.
333 11th Ave.
Columbus, OH 43201
(614) 421-2121

OKLAHOMA
Attorney Grievance
State Office:
General Counsel
Oklahoma Bar Center
1901 N. Lincoln Blvd.
P.O. Box 53036
State Capitol Station
Oklahoma City, OK 73152
(405) 524-2365

Client Security Fund
(Address, telephone same as for
Attorney Grievance.)

Fee Arbitration
Complaints referred for local hearing.

(Address, telephone same as for
Attorney Grievance.)

OREGON
Attorney Grievance
State Office:
General Counsel
Oregon State Bar
1776 S.W. Madison St.
Portland, OR 97205
(503) 224-4280

OREGON (continued)
Client Security Fund
Committee on Clients' Security Fund
(Address, telephone same as for
Attorney Grievance.)

Fee Arbitration
Complaints referred for local hearing.

(Address, telephone same as for
Attorney Grievance.)

PENNSYLVANIA
Attorney Grievance
State Office:
Chief Disciplinary Counsel
Disciplinary Board of the Supreme
   Court
300 N. Second St.
Commerce Bldg., 3rd Fl.
Harrisburg, PA 17101
(717) 232-7525

Client Security Fund
Supreme Court of Pennsylvania
1414 Three Penn Center Plaza
Philadelphia, PA 19102
(215) 496-4500

Fee Arbitration
Complaints referred for local hearing.
(Address same as for Attorney
Grievance.)
(717) 238-6715

PUERTO RICO
Attorney Grievance
Commission for Professional Ethics
Puerto Rico Bar Assn.
P.O. Box 1900
San Juan, PR 00903
(809) 721-3358

Client Security Fund
(Address, telephone same as for Attorney
Grievance.)

Fee Arbitration
None.

RHODE ISLAND
Attorney Grievance
State Office:
Disciplinary Board
Supreme Court Bldg.
250 Benefit St., 9th Fl.
Providence, RI 02903
(401) 277-3270

Client Security Fund
Rhode Island Bar Assn.
1804 Industrial Bank Bldg.
Providence, RI 02903
(401) 421-5740

Fee Arbitration
Complaints referred to the disciplinary
board for local hearing.

Chief Disciplinary Counsel of Rhode
   Island Supreme Court
(Address, telephone same as for
Attorney Grievance.)

SOUTH CAROLINA
Attorney Grievance
State Office:
Board of Commissioners on Grievances
   and Discipline
P.O. Box 11330
Columbia, SC 29211
(803) 758-7172

Client Security Fund
Director of Public Services
South Carolina Bar
P.O. Box 11039
Columbia, SC 29211
(803) 799-6653

Fee Arbitration
Complaints referred for local hearing.

Resolution of Fee Dispute Program
(Address, telephone same as Client
Security Fund.)

SOUTH DAKOTA
Attorney Grievance
State Office:
State Bar of South Dakota
222 E. Capitol
Pierre, SD 57501
(605) 224-7554

Client Security Fund
(Address, telephone same as for
Attorney Grievance.)

Fee Arbitration
Complaints referred for local hearing.

(Address, telephone same as for
Attorney Grievance.)

TENNESSEE
Attorney Grievance
State Office:
Disciplinary Board of the Supreme
  Court
The Oaks Office Tower
1101 Kermit Dr., Ste. 405
Nashville, TN 37217
(615) 361-7500

Client Security Fund
Tennessee Bar Assn.
3622 West End Ave.
Nashville, TN 37205
(615) 383-7421

Fee Arbitration
State bar refers cases to local fee
arbitration where available.

(Address, telephone same as Client
Security Fund.)

TEXAS
Attorney Grievance
State Office:
State Bar of Texas
Texas Law Center
1414 Colorado St.
P.O. Box 12487
Capitol Station
Austin, TX 78711
(512) 475-6202

TEXAS *(continued)*
Client Security Fund
(Address, telephone same as for Attorney
Grievance.)

Fee Arbitration
State bar refers cases to local fee
arbitration where available.

(Address, telephone same as for
Attorney Grievance.)

UTAH
Attorney Grievance
State Office:
Bar Counsel
Utah State Bar
425 E. First South
Salt Lake City, UT 84111
(801) 531-9077

Client Security Fund
(Address, telephone same as for Attorney
Grievance.)

Fee Arbitration
Complaints referred for local hearing.

(Address, telephone same as for
Attorney Grievance.)

VERMONT
Attorney Grievance
State Office:
P.O. Box 569
7 Washington St.
Middlebury, VT 05753
(802) 388-7933

Client Security Fund
Vermont Bar Assn.
P.O. Box 100
Montpelier, VT 05602
(802) 223-2020

Fee Arbitration
Complaints referred for local hearing.

(Address same as Client Security Fund.)
(802) 388-7966

VIRGINIA
Attorney Grievance
State Office:
Bar Counsel
Virginia State Bar
700 E. Main St., Ste. 1622
Richmond, VA 23219
(804) 786-2061

Client Security Fund
(Address, telephone same as for
Attorney Grievance.)

Fee Arbitration
State bar refers cases to local fee
arbitration where available.

(Address, telephone same as for
Attorney Grievance.)

VIRGIN ISLANDS
Attorney Grievance
Virgin Islands Bar Assn.
P.O. Box 6580
32 Norre Gade
Saint Thomas, VI 00801
(809) 774-8403

Client Security Fund
None.

Fee Arbitration
None.

WASHINGTON
Attorney Grievance
State Office:
General Counsel
Washington State Bar Assn.
505 Madison St.
Seattle, WA 98104
(206) 622-6026

Client Security Fund
(Address, telephone same as for Attorney
Grievance.)

WASHINGTON *(continued)*
Fee Arbitration
Complaints referred for local hearing.

Fee Arbitration Committee
(Address, telephone same as for
Attorney Grievance.)

WEST VIRGINIA
Attorney Grievance
State Office:
West Virginia State Bar
E-400 State Capitol
Charleston, WV 25305
(304) 348-2456

Client Security Fund
(Address same as for Attorney
Grievance.)
(304) 346-8414

Fee Arbitration
None.

WISCONSIN
Attorney Grievance
State Office:
Board of Attorneys Professional
    Responsibility
Supreme Court of Wisconsin
110 E. Main St., Rm. 406
Madison, WI 53703
(608) 267-7274

Client Security Fund
State Bar of Wisconsin
P.O. 7158
Madison, WI 53707
(608) 257-3838

Fee Arbitration
Complaints referred for local hearing.

(Address, telephone same as Client
Security Fund.)

WYOMING
Attorney Grievance
State Office:
Grievance Committee
Wyoming State Bar
P.O. Box 109
Cheyenne, WY 82003
(307) 632-9061

Client Security Fund
(Address, telephone same as for
Attorney Grievance.)

Fee Arbitration
Complaints referred for local hearing.

(Address, telephone same as for
Attorney Grievance.)

HALT

HALT — An Organization of Americans for Legal Reform is a national nonpartisan public interest group of more than 100,000 members. It is dedicated to the principle that all people in the United States should be able to dispose of their legal affairs in a simple, affordable and equitable manner. HALT works to:

- Increase awareness that people can — and should be able to — handle their own civil legal affairs.

- Reduce the number of cases that clog our courts by eliminating unnecessary litigation and promoting alternative ways of resolving disputes.

- Simplify the civil court system and its procedures and make it accountable to the public.

To accomplish these goals, HALT publishes its *Citizens Legal Manuals* series and a variety of one-page guides to the basic principles and procedures of the legal system. These materials are all written in simple, easy-to-understand language. They include step-by-step "how to" instructions, lists of other resources and explanations of the law and citizens' rights and responsibilities.

HALT's quarterly newsletter, *Americans for Legal Reform*, is the nation's top publication of legal reform news, analysis and opinion. It keeps members informed about major legal reform efforts and what they can do to help. Regular features include book reviews, a Legal Advisor column and legislative updates.

In state legislatures and the U.S. Congress, HALT supports:

- Reforming "Unauthorized Practice of Law" (UPL) by which state bar associations forbid nonlawyers to handle routine, uncontested matters.

- Public participation in open and effective procedures for disciplining judges and lawyers and settling disputes between lawyers and clients.

- Efficient and equitable no-fault systems of compensating victims for their injuries — whether from auto collisions, product or environmental hazards or medical malpractice.

- Standard do-it-yourself forms for routine, uncontested divorces, wills and other legal matters.

- Plain-language standards for all legal documents.

- Simplified probate procedures, eliminating unnecessary lawyer-involvement in probate and prohibiting probate lawyers from collecting a percentage of the estate rather than an hourly or flat fee.

- Requiring mediation, arbitration or other out-of-court methods of resolving a wide variety of disputes.

All HALT's activities are funded by member contributions. Since its founding in 1978, HALT has been instrumental in achieving reforms in several states from Maine to California, but much more needs to be done. You can help by joining HALT or enrolling a friend. Your contributions are tax deductible. For further information, write:

HALT, Inc.
201 Massachusetts Ave., N.E., Suite 312
Washington, D.C. 20002
(202) 546-4258

NOTES